Sketches from Scripture

Sketches from Scripture

A new collection of drama resources for churches, schools and youth groups

DEREK HAYLOCK

National Society/Church House Publishing
Church House, Great Smith Street, London SW1P 3NZ

ISBN 0 7151 4812 5

Published 1992 by the National Society and Church House Publishing

© Derek Haylock 1992

PERFORMING RIGHTS

Cover design by Bill Bruce

Printed in England by The Ludo Press Ltd, London SW18 3DG

CONTENTS

SKETCHES FROM SCRIPTURE

A new collection of drama resources for churches, schools and youth groups

This collection of dramatic sketches is a successor to *Acts for Apostles* and *Drama for Disciples* (National Society/CHP). The collection shows a variety of ways in which drama can be used in the service of the gospel, by church drama groups, youth groups, and with children. Certainly some of the material here could be useful in schools as a means of helping young people to identify with the stories from the Bible. All the sketches in this collection are clearly based on passages from the Bible.

The pieces were written originally for use in my home church, Surrey Chapel. This is a large and lively Free Church in the lovely cathedral city of Norwich, taking its name from the original location in Surrey Street. Occasionally we use our adult drama group, the Surrey Fringe, to provide a fresh angle to a familiar Bible story, with pieces like 'A Grave Business' and 'Telephone Conversation'. Sometimes members of the youth groups might contribute a piece requiring fairly limited acting abilities and very little learning of lines, such as 'The Prodigal Daughter' to a special family service. Also included in the collection is a serial play in five episodes, 'The Voyage of the Good Ship Crispin', for performance to children, designed to introduce some important concepts to be followed up in a teaching scheme on the life of Simon Peter. We also encourage children in our young church to improvise drama, as in 'Odd One In', as a basis for discussion and further Bible-based teaching.

Many of these pieces make use of humour as a vehicle for making contact with the audience, as indeed did Jesus himself. It has been liberating for us to discover that it's OK to laugh in church!

In making these sketches available to a wider audience, I have retained many local references in the expectation that others will adapt and modify the material to suit their own circumstances. I have been much encouraged to hear from a number of churches and schools who have found the material in the earlier collections useful. Please let me know how you get on with *Sketches from Scripture*.

Quotations from the Bible are taken from the *New International Version*, published in Great Britain by Hodder & Stoughton.

DEREK HAYLOCK

With special acknowledgments and thanks to four first-rate actors and valued friends—Gill, Jenny, Rachel and Tony—and other occasional members of the Surrey Fringe.

THE CHRISTMAS LECTURE

Bible Base: Matthew 1.18–25; Luke 2.1–7; John 1.4–14; Hebrews 1.2.

Introduction: This piece aims to highlight the possibility of Christmas being dominated by trivia, instead of by the amazing miracle of the birth of the Son of God at Bethlehem. It requires very little preparation and practically no learning of lines.

Cast: Chairperson, Secretary, Lecturer.

(For most of the sketch, the three members of the cast are seated behind a small table, with the Lecturer in the middle. The Secretary appears to take minutes throughout the lecture. When the interruptions occur these are done in audible stage whispers, which become more and more forceful as the lecture proceeds. For some reason it appears to be more effective for the Lecturer to adopt a mock East European accent.

The Chairperson and Secretary enter and busy themselves preparing the stage and lighting, improvising some dialogue as appropriate, along the following lines.)

Chair You deal with the lighting, William, and I'll get the seating arranged on the stage, OK?

Secretary Fair enough, after all you are supposed to be the chairman.

Chair Person, William. Chairperson.

Secretary There, how's that? Lighting OK?

Chair Fine. I think he should be here any minute.

Secretary Oh, goodie, goodie! I do enjoy these Christmas lectures. I hope it will be as good as last year's. *(Joining the Chairperson on the stage.)*

Chair I wonder if anyone will come to hear it?

Secretary Mmm, I wonder. *(They look at the audience, do a double-take, and jump with surprise!)* Ooh, where did they come from? Right, shall I go and see if he's here then?

Chair Yes, I think it's time to get going. *(Secretary goes offstage to meet the Lecturer, brings him onstage, and introduces him to the Chairperson; they all take their seats. The Chairperson stands.)*

Chair Ladies and gentlemen, and . . . . *(looking round the audience)* oh, yes, the vicar–welcome to the first lecture in this year's series of annual Christmas lectures, which, as you know, is the series of annual lectures which we have, once a year . . . annually, at Christmas . . . each year. Our speaker this year is Dr Otto Liebfraumilch, the vice-president of the Society for the Preservation of European Ancient Customs. And his subject is 'What is Christmas All About?' So, please give a very warm welcome to our speaker. *(Leads applause, with the Secretary and, hopefully, the audience, joining in. The Lecturer stands, as the Chairperson sits, shuffles notes and begins.)*

Lecturer What is Christmas all about?

Secretary *(hand shoots up like a child at school)* Sir, sir, I know . . .

Chair *(whispering behind speaker's back)* Quiet, Secretary . . . listen to the lecture.

Lecturer *(looking a little displeased by the interruption)* Christmas. What is it all about? What is its true meaning and significance? Where can we find the real spirit of Christmas? In this first lecture I would like to focus your attention on . . . the Christmas tree. Now the custom of using evergreens during the winter as religious symbols and decorations dates back to pagan times. The Romans, for example, decorated their homes with evergreen branches in memory of their God Saturn. But the use of a young spruce tree as part of the Christian festival in Britain goes back only about one hundred and fifty years.

(The Chairperson and Secretary begin to look at each other a little anxiously behind the lecturer's back.)

In fact, this custom originated in Germany. Martin Luther, 1483 to 1546, introduced the fir tree to people's homes and used a candlelit tree to represent the starry sky. By 1605 it is reported that the townspeople of Strasbourg were setting up these trees in their homes at Christmas and decorating them with apples, sweets, paper roses and . . .

Secretary *(interrupting)* Excuse me, but shouldn't you be talking about Bethlehem, not Strasbourg?

Lecturer Bethlehem? Where is that?

Chair You know, Bethlehem in Judea. Where Jesus was born.

Secretary It's near Jerusalem.

Lecturer *(tetchily)* Christmas trees do not grow in Jerusalem. Foolish person. *(Returning to the lecture.)* As I was saying. The Christmas tree. Christmas trees were introduced into this country in the nineteenth century. Mainly responsible for making them popular in Britain was Prince Albert, the young German husband of Queen Victoria.

Secretary *(tugging at the Lecturer's sleeve)* Tell them about Mary and Joseph, not Albert and Victoria.

Lecturer Who are these Mary and Joseph? Did they have a Christmas tree?

Chair No, of course not.

Lecturer Then they are not relevant. *(Returning to the lecture.)* To return to my subject. The Christmas tree. Once the British aristocracy had adopted the custom of putting up fir trees at Christmas, others soon copied the idea.

Secretary What about the stable?

Lecturer Stable? No, they did not put Christmas trees in the stable. It would frighten the horses. *(Chuckles.)*

Secretary No, I mean the stable where Mary had to go with Joseph to have her baby . . .

Chair . . . because there was no room for them at the inn . . .

Lecturer And this stable, what was it made from?

Secretary Wood, I suppose.

Lecturer And where does wood come from?

Secretary Trees, of course.

Lecturer Precisely. Trees. *(Resuming lecture.)* And at this time of year, our thoughts turn to . . . the Christmas tree. Before long the custom had developed in the nineteenth century of decorating Christmas trees with small candles, cakes, gingerbread, fruit and sweets.

Secretary Tell them about the baby Jesus.

Lecturer I was just coming to that. A common practice in Victorian times was to put a model of the baby Jesus on top of . . . the Christmas tree.

Chair No, that's not what we mean. Tell them about the angel . . .

Lecturer Ah, yes, the angel. Later on, some people took to putting a model of an angel with golden wings at the top of their Christmas tree. Still later this became a fairy with a wand and a tinsel dress.

Chair I mean, tell them about what the angel said. About Jesus coming to save people from their sins.

Lecturer *(trying to press on with the lecture)* It was the usual practice to leave the sweets and fruit on the tree . . .

Secretary The Son of God being born as a human baby . . .

Lecturer . . . to give to the children on Twelfth Night, so that they would not be too sad . . .

Chair God, actually stepping into his own creation . . .

Lecturer . . . when Christmas was all over and the tree had to be taken down. Nowadays trees are seen everywhere at Christmas. The most famous tree is the one erected every year in Trafalgar Square . . .

Secretary We're talking about the most amazing miracle in the history of the world . . .

Lecturer . . . since 1947, a gift from the good people of Oslo to the people of London, as a sign of friendship and peace. Many people come to London at this time of year to see the lights . . .

Chair Tell about the light that shone in the darkness . . .

Lecturer . . . and to see this famous tree. They gather round it to sing the traditional Christmas carols. Here, then, in the humble Christmas tree we see something of the meaning of Christmas. People coming together, sharing gifts, music, friendship, warmth, even love. Peace, and goodwill to all. Simple, homely, traditional values, yes, but none the worse for that.

Chair *(whispering to Secretary behind Lecturer's back)* Where's the light switch? *(The Secretary points and the Chairperson surreptitiously picks up a Bible and starts to leave as this speech proceeds.)*

Lecturer Because when all is said and done, Christmas is all about traditions . . . and in the forthcoming lectures in this series I will talk about other traditional Christmas customs—the turkey dinner, Christmas crackers, the Christmas pantomime, the *Cannon and Ball Christmas Special*—each of which speaks to us in some way about the true meaning of Christmas. *(Pauses, and shuffles papers, looking for something.)*

Chair *(now at edge of stage, reading from the Bible)* The word of God says: in the past God has spoken to us through the prophets at many times and in various ways *(the Secretary looks up as the Chair begins reading, puts down papers and goes across to join the Chair)* . . . but in these last days he has spoken to us by his Son . . .

Secretary *(looking over the Chair's shoulder, and reading)* . . . whom he appointed heir of all things, and through whom he made the universe. *(They continue towards exit.)*

Lecturer Finally, to help us remember what Christmas is all about we can make some simple models of Christmas trees from green card, to decorate the mantelpiece. Just cut out two shapes like this ...

Secretary *(calling across towards the Lecturer, not shouting, but very determined)* The Word became flesh and lived for a while among us.

Lecturer ...make slits at the top of one and the bottom of the other ...

Chair *(reaching the exit where the light switch is located)* In him was life, and that life was the light of men.

Lecturer Fix them together with glue, sprinkle on some glitter ...

Secretary The light shines in the darkness, but the darkness has not understood it.

Lecturer *(producing a model Christmas tree from under the table in true* Blue Peter *fashion)* Here is one I prepared earlier ...

(Chair and Secretary switch off the lights, leaving the Lecturer in darkness.)

RESPONSES TO JESUS

Bible Base: Matthew 1.18–2.12; Luke 1.26–2.38.

Introduction: This is a script for a fairly traditional and serious Nativity Play, allowing participation by as many children as are available. It is expected that the main characters will be in costume, and that they will eventually form a traditional tableau around the manger. Apart from the Narrators, who, of course, will read their parts, there are just a few simple lines to be learnt by the main characters and by the Chorus. The particular thrust of the play is its focus on the variety of responses to Jesus, with the final challenge to the audience to consider how they themselves will respond to him.

Cast: Narrators 1 and 2, Mary, Joseph, Gabriel, Innkeeper, Shepherds 1 and 2, Wise Men 1 and 2, Herod, Anna, Simeon, Chorus (all available children).

(You will need a traditional manger, centre stage, with a doll representing the baby Jesus out of sight inside. All available children, including the main characters, form the Chorus. They are in two groups, referred to as Chorus A and Chorus B, either side of the stage, facing inwards. Narrator 1 stands facing the audience on the same side as Chorus A, and Narrator 2 likewise with Chorus B. Chorus A includes Mary, Joseph, Anna, and the Shepherds. Chorus B includes Gabriel, the Innkeeper, Herod, Simeon and the Wise Men. The main characters come forward for their contributions, then return to their places in the Chorus. The contributions by the Chorus should be practised very thoroughly so that they speak with one voice, pausing in the places indicated by . . ., and stressing the same words.)

Narrator 1 He was born nearly two thousand years ago, to a young woman and her carpenter husband, in a small town near Jerusalem.

Narrator 2 But his birth was an event which was to change the world.

Narrator 1 Even in his infancy,

Narrator 2 as it would be in his adult life,

Narrator 1 They reacted to him in many ways.

Narrator 2 Some of those who were there show us how they responded...

Narrator 1 to the one they called ...

Chorus Jesus!

> *(Mary and Gabriel step forward from opposite sides: appropriate action.)*

Narrator 1 In the sixth month, God sent the angel Gabriel to Nazareth, a town in Galilee, to a virgin pledged to be married to a man named Joseph.

Narrator 2 The virgin's name was Mary.

Gabriel Do not be afraid, Mary, you have found favour with God. You will give birth to a son, and you are to give him the name Jesus.

Chorus Give him the name ...Jesus.

Gabriel He will be great and will be called the Son of the Most High. *(Returns to Chorus.)*

Chorus He will be great ...and will be called ...the Son of the Most High.

Mary He was just an ordinary-looking baby. But the things that happened later made me realise. The angel was right. My son was someone very special.

Narrator 1 And his mother Mary treasured all these things in her heart.

> *(Mary steps back, as Joseph and Gabriel step forward from opposite sides.)*

Narrator 2 An angel of the Lord appeared to Joseph in a dream.

Gabriel Do not be afraid to take Mary home as your wife, because what is conceived in her is from the Holy Spirit. She will give birth to a son and you are to give him the name Jesus, because he will save his people from their sins. *(Gabriel returns to Chorus.)*

Chorus Give him the name ...Jesus.

Joseph So we called him Jesus. This means Saviour. And we believed what the angel said—that somehow our son Jesus was going to save people from their sins.

Narrator 1 All this took place to fulfil what the Lord had said through the prophet.

Narrator 2 The virgin will be with child and will give birth to a son, and they will call him Immanuel, which means:

Chorus *(strongly, three words separated)* God ...with ...us.

> *(Mary and Joseph now come together and take their places beside the manger. Mary lifts the baby out of the crib, wraps a blanket round it, returns it, then they remain static.)*

Narrator 1 While they were in Bethlehem, the time came for the baby to be born, and Mary gave birth to her firstborn, a son.

Narrator 2 She wrapped him in strips of cloth and placed him in a manger, because there was no room for them in the inn.

Innkeeper *(stepping forward from the Chorus)* That was such a busy time for us. The town was packed out with visitors come for the census. I didn't have time to stop and ask questions.

Chorus A No room.

Chorus B For Jesus.

Chorus A No room.

Chorus B At Christmas. *(Innkeeper returns to the Chorus, as the Shepherds step forward.)*

Narrator 1 There were shepherds living out in the fields nearby, keeping watch over their flocks at night. *(Gabriel steps forward to address the Shepherds, who react appropriately.)*

Narrator 2 An angel of the Lord appeared to them.

Narrator 1 The glory of the Lord shone around them.

Narrator 2 They were terrified.

Gabriel Do not be afraid. I bring you good news of great joy that will be for all the people. Today in the town of David a Saviour has been born to you. He is Christ the Lord.

Chorus He is Christ the Lord!

Gabriel This will be a sign to you. You will find a baby wrapped in strips of cloth, and lying in a manger.

Narrator 1 Suddenly, a great company of the heavenly host appeared with the angel, praising God, and saying:

Chorus A Glory to God in the highest!

Chorus B Glory to God in the highest!

Chorus Glory to God in the highest!

Narrator 2 And on earth, peace to those on whom his favour rests. *(Gabriel steps back.)*

Shepherd 1 We went at once to Bethlehem.

Shepherd 2 And we found Mary and Joseph in a stable.

Shepherd 1 And the baby lying in a manger.

Shepherd 2 It was just as the angel had said.

Shepherd 1 And then we believed.

Shepherd 2 This was our Saviour.

Shepherd 1 Christ the Lord.

(Shepherds kneel around the manger.)

Chorus Jesus . . . is . . . Lord!

Narrator 1 The shepherds returned.

Narrator 2 Glorifying and praising God for all the things they had seen and heard.

(Shepherds return to their places, with appropriate action. Wise Men step forward.)

Narrator 1 After Jesus was born in Bethlehem, during the reign of King Herod, wise men from the East came to Jerusalem.

Wise Man 1 Where is the one who has been born king of the Jews? We saw his star in the East and have come to worship him. *(Herod steps forward.)*

Narrator 2 King Herod called the wise men secretly, found out from them the exact time the star had appeared, and sent them to Bethlehem.

Herod Go and make a careful search for the child. As soon as you find him, report to me, so that I too may go and worship him.

Chorus *(questioning)* Go . . . and worship him?

Herod *(aside to audience, in an evil voice)* So that I can dispose of the wretched child as quickly as possible! *(Returns to place in the Chorus.)*

Wise Man 1 The star led us to Bethlehem.

Wise Man 2 And when we found him we were overjoyed.

(Appropriate action, as the Wise Men kneel around the manger.)

Narrator 1 On coming to the house, they saw the child with his mother, Mary.

Narrator 2 And they bowed down and worshipped him.

Narrator 1 Then they opened their treasures and presented him with gifts.

Chorus Gold . . . frankincense . . . myrrh.

(Pause, then the Wise Men return to their places in the Chorus, Anna steps forward, Mary and Joseph pick up the baby from the manger and walk across to greet her.)

Narrator 2 Later, Joseph and Mary took the child to the Temple in Jerusalem to present him to the Lord. There they met a very old widow, a prophetess, named Anna, who never left the Temple, but worshipped God day and night.

(Mary hands the baby to Anna.)

Anna When I saw the child I gave thanks to God. I knew then that he had at last sent our Saviour into the world.

Chorus A God so loved the world . . .

Chorus B He gave his only Son.

> *(Anna returns the baby to Mary, and takes her place in the Chorus, as Simeon steps forward. Mary and Joseph walk across to greet him, again handing the baby over to him when they meet.)*

Narrator 1 And there was a man in Jerusalem called Simeon. He was a good, devout man, waiting for Israel to be saved.

Narrator 2 It had been revealed to him by the Holy Spirit that he would not die before he saw the Lord's promised Messiah. When the parents brought in the child Jesus, Simeon took him in his arms and praised God.

Simeon As I held him in my arms, I knew great joy.

Narrator 1 Because God had at last sent his promised one.

Simeon And I knew great sadness.

Narrator 2 Because he would save us only through his suffering and death.

Simeon My eyes have seen your salvation. *(Simeon returns the baby to Mary and takes his place back in the Chorus, walking very slowly.)*

Chorus Our eyes . . . have seen . . . your salvation.

Narrator 1 Sovereign Lord, as you have promised, you now dismiss your servant in peace.

> *(Mary and Joseph take centre stage, standing behind the manger, heads held up. Mary holds the baby slightly away from her as though inviting the audience to respond. The other characters gradually take up positions in a final tableau as the Narrator concludes.)*

Narrator 2 The angel said he was the Son of the most high God, the one who would save people from their sins. *(Gabriel steps forward, stands gesturing towards Mary.)* Mary and Joseph trusted and believed this. *(Mary and Joseph now look down in wonder at the child in her arms.)* The angels told the shepherds that his birth was good news of great joy, because a saviour had been born. *(Shepherds come forward and kneel in worship.)* The shepherds listened, obeyed, believed, and went on their way rejoicing. *(Innkeeper steps forward and takes up position on one side of the stage with back towards Mary and Joseph.)* The innkeeper was too busy and had no room for Jesus. *(Wise Men step forward and kneel in worship.)* The wise men recognised him as a king, and gave him their costliest treasures. *(Herod steps forward, looks* *angrily at the child, and takes up position on opposite side from the Innkeeper, with his back towards Mary and Joseph.)* Herod saw him as a threat and tried to have him destroyed. *(Anna and Simeon step forward and stand either side of Mary and Joseph.)* Old Anna and old Simeon knew they would die in peace because they had seen in Jesus the promise of God for salvation, fulfilled.

Narrator 1 And what of us today? Will we ignore him? Have no time for him? Reject him? See him as a threat?

Narrator 2 Or will we recognise him?

Narrator 1 Trust him.

Narrator 2 Obey him.

Narrator 1 Believe him.

Narrator 2 Worship him.

Narrator 2 And go on our way rejoicing, because Jesus, the Saviour of the world, is our Saviour.

Narrator 1 How will we respond to Jesus this Christmas? *(Remainder of the Chorus come forward and kneel before the manger, to complete the tableau.)*

THE PRODIGAL DAUGHTER

Bible Base: Luke 15.11–32.

Introduction: Even though this features two daughters rather than two sons, there's nothing very original about the idea in this sketch of a modern-day version of the familiar story from Luke 15. However, there is a surprise in store for the audience when, towards the end of the piece, one of the Narrators tries to change the ending. This serves to highlight the astounding truth of this parable, our heavenly Father's willingness to forgive us in spite of our disobedience and self-centredness.

Cast: The father, Tracey and Sharon, his daughters, Narrators 1 and 2, various 'friends', supermarket manager, landlord.

(Two narrators stand at the back of the stage, one either side. Narrator 2 speaks in the style of a Radio 1 disc-jockey. Narrator 1, by contrast, is very much Radio 4. Appropriate action to be improvised throughout by actors. Our local references, for instance to Norfolk and the A11, can, of course, be changed to suit your own situation.)

Narrator 1 We present the story of the prodigal daughter.

Narrator 2 Hang about. Shouldn't that be the prodigal son?

Narrator 1 *(stage whisper)* We're a bit short of male actors.

Narrator 2 Fair enough. Equal opportunities and all that stuff. What does it mean anyway?

Narrator 1 What?

Narrator 2 This 'prodigal' bit.

Narrator 1 *(pretending to know, but not fooling anyone)* Well, you know, it comes from the Latin: prod- dig- all. It means, well, prodigal, I suppose.

Narrator 2 You don't know either, do you.

Narrator 1 Of course I do. *(Turns back on Narrator 2, takes out a pocket dictionary, quickly looks through the pages and reads in a knowing voice)* It means—how can I put it?—sort of 'wasteful of one's means', um, 'squandering', 'lavish'—actually.

Tracey *(calling from off-stage)* Can we get on with it, please?

Narrator 1 OK. Scene one.

Narrator 2 This guy in Norfolk, right. He's a rich farmer. *(Father enters: mimes appropriately.)* Really loaded. Know what I mean? Big farm, acres of turnips, carrots, cabbages, oilseed rape, all that green stuff, right. Making serious money. You get the picture?

Narrator 1 The farmer had two daughters.

(They enter as their names are mentioned, curtsey and greet their father.)

Narrator 2 Tracey . . . and Sharon.

Narrator 1 They were both elegant, charming, talented, exceptionally beautiful.

Narrator 2 *(gesturing towards Tracey and Sharon)* Is this right?

Narrator 1 *(stage whisper)* We're a bit short of elegant, charming, talented, and exceptionally beautiful actresses.

Narrator 2 Fair enough.

Narrator 1 Our story commences one lovely summer's day in the idyllic setting of the family's Norfolk farmhouse. Skylarks were singing their merry tune high in the sky, the fruit on the apple trees was slowly ripening in the golden summer sun, cornflowers held their proud heads high along the hedgerows, and . . .

Tracey Get on with it . . . please!

Narrator 2 Right, the plot. *(The actors mime appropriately— it all happens very quickly.)* Tracey fed up with country life. In a sulk. Goes to Dad. Demands her share of the family fortune. Wants to go to London to live her own life. Mega tantrum. Dad gives in. Sharon thinks it a disgrace. Tracey takes the money, makes rude gesture to Sharon *(not too rude, please!)*, packs bags and makes tracks for the big city.

Narrator 1 Scene two. London. *(Father and Sharon leave stage, Tracey wanders around looking at the sights.)*

Narrator 2 The big city. Bright lights, trendy, where the action is, life in the fast lane. Discos, parties, filofax, all that stuff. You get the picture?

Narrator 1 Tracey soon settled into the high life of the big city. She made friends quickly—and spent her money with abandon to impress them. She threw a big party for all her new friends. *(Friends enter, mime disco.)*

Narrator 2 Free cokes and crisps all round. Disco music, flashing lights, hours of fun. Then goodnight, Trace, cheers, see yer.

(The friends wave and exit; then come straight back on again.)

Narrator 1 The next night she threw another party, although she was a bit worried when she checked her purse.

Narrator 2 Free cokes all round—but no crisps. Disco music, flashing lights, hours of fun. Then goodnight, Trace, cheers, see yer. *(The friends wave and exit, then come straight back on again.)*

Narrator 1 The next night she threw another party. But her money was running out.

Narrator 2 Disco music, flashing lights, hours of fun. But no free cokes or crisps. Friends disappointed. Goodnight, Trace, cheers, see yer. *(They wave and exit.)*

Narrator 1 The next night she threw another party. But no-one came. She wandered lonely through the dark streets of the big city. She checked her purse. She was broke. *(Tracey opens her purse, turns it upside down, one coin drops out.)*

Narrator 2 Well, nearly broke.

Narrator 1 She gave her last 10p to a deserving cause. *(Tracey picks up the coin, leaves the stage and hands it to someone appropriate in the audience.)* She wandered back to the solitude of her flat in the Fulham Road and cried her way through the night. From here on it was downhill all the way.

Narrator 2 Fate had put the skids under Tracey's life.

Narrator 1 She took a job at a checkout in Tescos, but got the sack for being late. *(Tracey dawdles across the stage, is confronted by an angry manager, looking at the time, who gives her a sack and signals that she is dismissed.)*

Narrator 2 Her landlord threw her out of her flat for not paying the rent. *(She wanders across to the other side of the stage, where the landlord confronts her—puts out a hand demanding payment. Tracey shakes her head. The landlord signals that she must go.)*

Narrator 1 The following week she slept in the sack under the Hammersmith flyover. *(Tracey curls up inside the sack in a corner of the stage.)*

Narrator 2 Life had taken a turn for the worse.

Narrator 1 Her sweet dream of freedom had turned sour.

Narrator 2 Hungry, miserable, homeless, penniless. You get the picture?

Narrator 1 Then suddenly Tracey comes to her senses.

Narrator 2 She's been a fool.

Tracey I've been a fool! *(She leaps up dramatically, looks resolute and begins to walk round the audience, on her way home.)*

Narrator 1 Even the women who pick the cabbages on her father's farm have a better life than this, she thought.

Narrator 2 Mega-regrets. Time for action, going-home-wise.

Narrator 1 Scene three. Meanwhile . . .

Narrator 2 Back on the farm. *(Father enters, takes position centre stage and looks out into the distance.)*

Narrator 1 As he had done every day since she had left home, Tracey's father gazed longingly down the A11, with the same old question running through his mind . . .

Narrator 2 . . . Will they ever make it dual-carriageway?

Narrator 1 *(ignoring this remark)* Will she ever come home again?

Narrator 2 *(sings)* 'Will she no come back again?'

Narrator 1 And then in the distance he saw someone approaching. *(Father reacts appropriately.)* Could it be? Surely not! Yes. It was! He called Sharon. *(Sharon enters.)* Come quickly! Look, our Tracey is coming home!
(Tracey reaches the stage and approaches the father, who stands with arms open wide to greet her.)

Tracey I'm sorry, Dad.

Narrator 1 The father opened wide his arms to greet her, and said . . .
(During the next bit of narration the three actors on stage and Narrator 1 look taken aback, and gradually move towards and form a group around Narrator 2.)

Narrator 2 *(forcefully)* How dare you come crawling back here after the way you treated us? You ungrateful little wretch. You had a decent home here, all that you could have wanted. And you walked out on us. Well, don't think you can just come home now as though nothing had happened. Oh no. You can just turn round and get back where you came from this moment. You took your money, you've had your chance, so just clear off . . .

Narrator 1 *(interrupting)* No! That's not right!

Narrator 2 Well, it's only what she deserves, isn't it?

Sharon Quite right.

Narrator 1 *(checking the script)* But doesn't the father actually want to forgive her? Look, he's been longing for her to come home. He even wants to have a party to celebrate, because his lost daughter has been found.

Sharon That's not fair!

Narrator 2 And quite unbelievable. You're not telling me that, after the way she's treated him, he's actually going to forgive her! Why would he do that?

Father, Tracey and Narrator 1 *(together, very deliberately)* Because he loves her!

TELEPHONE CONVERSATION

Bible Base: Luke 18.18–27; Matthew 19.16–26.

Introduction: It is often difficult or inappropriate to act out incidents which involve someone playing the part of the Lord Jesus. This sketch and the next *(A Grave Business)* deal with this problem by a couple of simple dramatic devices. This one recounts the story of the rich young ruler meeting the Lord Jesus by having the young man's mother talking to him over the telephone. The idea derives from the Maureen Lipman advertisements for British Telecom. The Jewish Momma and Poppa in this sketch are therefore depicted as rather stereotypical characters, but this is done with genuine love and admiration for the kind of Jewish humour which emanates from Jewish writers themselves. In fact, to be honest, all the humour in this piece has been lifted quite blatantly from Jewish authors like Rabbi Lionel Blue.

Cast: Momma, Poppa, Reader.

(Momma is seated at a table by a telephone, polishing her jewellery. She is the dominant partner in the marriage and very protective towards her son. Poppa lounges in an easy chair, reading a newspaper. He likes a quiet life. The telephone rings, Momma picks it up and is excited to discover that it is her boy, Sammy, calling her. Dotted lines like this . . . are used to indicate places in the script where Momma listens to what Sammy is saying.)

Momma Hello? . . . Sammy! Joseph, wake up, it's Samuel. *(Tearfully)* He's ringing his mother and it's not even her birthday! Is he not a good son to his poor old mother?

Poppa Tell him his Poppa says hello. And how much does he want?

Momma Your Poppa says hello, Sammy . . . *(To Poppa)* He says hello back. *(To Sammy)* Can we help you in some way? You need some money perhaps? . . . *(To Poppa)* He says he doesn't need any money. *(To Samuel)* Are you unwell, Sammy? You're upset about something, I know. Momma can always tell when you're upset. *(To Poppa)* He's upset about something, Joseph. Didn't I say I can always tell when he's upset?

Poppa *(not really listening)* Yes, dearest.

Momma Which new teacher is that, Sammy? ... *(To Poppa)* Your son's been talking to that new teacher from Nazareth.

Poppa Yes, dearest.

Momma And is he a good teacher, this Jesus? ... I see ... *(To Poppa)* The teacher says no-one is good except God alone.

Poppa For this he gets a living?

Momma And did you ask him a question, Sammy? ... *(To Poppa)* He asked him a question, Joseph.

Poppa Yes, dearest.

Momma And what was your question, Sammy? ... That is a good question, my boy. I am very proud of you for asking a question like that. *(To Poppa)* Joseph, our boy is a theologian. He asks the teacher what he must do to inherit eternal life. Is that not a good question he is asking?

Poppa Yes, dearest.

Momma Your father thinks it is a good question too, Sammy. *(Tearfully again)* I am such a proud mother. First my boy is telephoning me when it is not even my birthday, and now he is telling me he asks a clever question of the new teacher. So, what was his answer? ... You know the commandments. Huh! He is asking my son if he knows the commandments! Oy, oy, oy! *(To Poppa)* Do you hear that, Joseph?

Poppa Yes, dearest.

Momma And is that a good answer to our son's question?

Poppa Yes, dearest.

Momma No, Joseph, the answer is no, dearest. It is not a good answer to our son's question. *(To Samuel)* Sammy, my boy, have we not taught you to keep all the commandments since you were a little baby at your mother's knee? ... That's right ... Yes, of course you honour your father and mother ... No, you have not given false testimony ... No, of course you do not steal ... No, you have never committed murder ... er, only you can answer that one, Sammy. Your mother would be the last person to know, I'm sure ... So why are you upset? ... He said you still lack one thing? *(To Poppa)* Oy, oy, oy. Now the teacher is saying that our boy is lacking something?

Poppa He is very perceptive, this teacher from Nazareth. I have often thought that this boy of yours is lacking something.

Momma What can you be lacking, Sammy, my boy? You have a good home. You have all the money you need? You have plenty of clothes? Didn't your Momma buy you two new robes last Passover? ... *(To Poppa)* He says he's wearing the red one now. *(To Samuel)* So what is wrong with the blue one, Samuel? Didn't you like the blue one?

Poppa Just ask him what the teacher said he is lacking, Momma.

Momma So what is this thing you are lacking? ... What? ... Oy, oy, oy. He told you to do what? ... *(To Poppa)* This teacher from Nazareth is now telling our boy to sell everything he has and give to the poor.

Poppa This way he will not get many disciples.

Momma *(suddenly very anxious)* You haven't done that, have you, Sammy? Please tell me you haven't done that! ... Oh, good. *(Relieved)* Your Momma was very worried for a moment then. So, why are you so sad, Sammy? ... So, the teacher said you could have treasure in heaven if you followed him? Who needs treasure in heaven? You have all the treasure you want here, my boy ... And anyway why should you worry about inheriting eternal life? When Poppa dies you will inherit this house and the most thriving second-hand camel business in Jerusalem. And by the looks of him that shouldn't be too long. *(To Poppa)* Tell me, am I right, Poppa?

Poppa Yes, dearest.

Momma Your father says that I am right, Sammy. So just pull yourself together, my boy, and stop worrying your little head about heaven and eternal life and a teacher from Nazareth who hasn't got two shekels to rub together anyway ... Sammy? Are you there, Sammy? *(To Poppa)* Now he is ringing off, when I'm talking to him. Is that any way for a boy to treat his mother?

Poppa Yes, dearest.

(Momma returns to polishing her jewellery; Poppa is already immersed in his newspaper. The Reader appears to read the conclusion to the story.)

Reader When the young man heard what Jesus said to him, he went away sad, because he had great wealth. Then Jesus said to his disciples, 'I tell you the truth, it is hard for a rich man to enter the kingdom of heaven. Again I tell you, it is easier for a camel to go through the eye of a needle than for a rich man to enter the kingdom of God.' When the disciples heard this, they were greatly astonished and asked, 'Who then can be saved?' Jesus looked at them and said, 'With man this is impossible, but with God all things are possible.'

A GRAVE BUSINESS

Bible Base: John 11.1–43.

Introduction: This sketch tells the story of the raising of Lazarus from the dead. The problem of acting out a story involving Jesus is dealt with by inventing two characters who might have been present at the time of the incident–the undertakers who had been responsible for the burial of Lazarus–and then having Mary and Martha recount to them what happened. The names Eli and She-li were chosen to allow one of the undertakers to be played by a female actor.

Cast: Eli and She-li, Mary, Martha, Lazarus, Narrator.

(Eli and She-li are undertakers. One corner of the stage, with two chairs, represents their office. She-li is rather frivolous, and spends the early part of the conversation scribbling, trying to invent witty slogans for the firm. Eli is more serious and obviously worried about business. There is a small house in another corner of the stage, representing the home of Mary, Martha and Lazarus. If possible, the house should have a window with curtains drawn. Lazarus is concealed inside the house beforehand. Eli and She-li take their seats on one side of the stage. Mary and Martha enter carrying some white clothes, which they hang on a washing line outside their house, as they chat happily to each other, then disappear inside.)

Narrator *(standing and gesturing towards Eli and She-li)* In the Jerusalem office of their small firm of undertakers, Eli and She-li are worried about business. *(Exit.)*

Eli Business is not good, She-li. We must attract more customers, or we'll be looking for undertakers ourselves.

She-li The advertising is what we need, I tell you. With the witty slogan. Like: 'Eli and She-li, Undertakers. The dead centre of Jerusalem.'

Eli You should not be joking about this matter, She-li. This is a grave business.

She-li *(laughs)* Very good, brother! A grave business. Yes, that is very good. Or what about, 'Eli and She-li, undertakers–people are dying to be our customers.'

Eli Your levity is not fitting, She-li. Pass me the accounts.

She-li *(passing the accounts over)* I see those two sisters in Bethany have not yet settled their bill for the funeral of their brother.

Eli That is true. So we can rely on some shekels in the next day or two. Let me see, single tomb for Lazarus of Bethany, grade two, no extras, two hundred and twenty shekels.

She-li 'Come to Eli and She-li for a tomb with a view.'

Eli That was a strange business in Bethany. When I called at their house last week I could see that he was not long for this world.

She-li You are always having an eye for a potential customer, Eli.

Eli I told them they were wasting their time sending for that healer, what was his name? You know, the one who has been teaching in Galilee . . .

She-li Jesus of Nazareth?

Eli That was the man. I told them, if he was not there within two days he would be arriving too late.

She-li So?

Eli Well, he did not seem in any hurry. They sent a message Thursday last week that Lazarus was seriously ill. Come yesterday, he had still not turned up and Lazarus had been safely tucked up in one of our tombs for four days.

She-li They say he was a good friend of theirs.

Eli Some friend. Not even there in time for the funeral.

She-li But we were, eh, brother? Eli and She-li, always on time when others are late. Late? Get it? Oh well, never mind.

Eli Come with me, She-li. We will be going to Bethany to collect our shekels. I have some things to say to you about your attitude. First . . .

(They stand, as though leaving, and freeze. Narrator enters quickly, introduces next scene and exits.)

Narrator It was a couple of miles walk from Jerusalem to Bethany. Half an hour later Eli and She-li are outside the home of Mary and Martha *(gesturing towards the house)*, the two sisters of Lazarus.

(Eli and She-li come to life again, and Eli carries on as though he has been talking non-stop.)

Eli . . . and ninthly, I was not amused when we buried that dentist last month and you remarked in a very loud voice that he had filled his last cavity.

(Eli knocks on the door.)

Martha *(from inside)* Who's there?

Eli Eli and She-li.

She-li Undertakers.

Eli Please accept our apologies for intruding on your grief, good sisters, but there is the small matter of our account.

She-li Business is business.

(Martha comes out.)

Martha Oh that's all right. It's nice to see you.

She-li You look surprisingly cheerful.,

Martha You want us to settle our account?

Eli This does not usually make our customers cheerful.

Martha Two hundred shekels, wasn't it? *(Calls indoors)* Bring two hundred shekels to pay the man, Mary.

Mary *(from inside)* Yes, Martha.

Eli Two hundred and twenty actually. But to you . . . all right, call me a fool.

(Mary appears.)

She-li You were fond of this brother of yours?

(They laugh gently.)

Eli There is something the matter? The tomb is not satisfactory? You would like me to check it over? Make sure it is sealed properly?

Martha and Mary *(sharing the joke)* Sealed properly! *(They laugh out loud.)*

She-li Will someone please be telling us what is going on?

Martha Yes, of course, sorry. Well, you remember we sent for Jesus. Last Thursday, wasn't it, Mary?

Mary Yes, Martha.

Eli And we also know that he did not come, not even for the funeral.

She-li And your brother is dead and buried. This is a very funny joke?

Martha *(excitedly)* Well, he did come. Yesterday afternoon. And I went out to meet him, didn't I, Mary?

Mary Yes, Martha.

Martha Look, I wrote it all down in my diary to make sure I would remember all the details. *(Referring to notes as necessary— speaking very excitedly, the story just pouring out.)* Right. I went out to meet Jesus as he was approaching the house, to warn him that Lazarus was already dead. Mary stayed in the house. I was ever so upset, as you can imagine. I shouted at him. 'If you had been here in time, Lord, my brother would not have died!' but then I thought that sounded a bit rude, so I told him that I still believed that his Father in heaven would give him whatever he asked for. And do you know, he just calmly said: 'Your brother will rise to life.' I thought he meant rise to life on the last day, but he just said *(reads this carefully)* 'I am the resurrection and the life. Whoever believes in me will live, even though he dies. And whoever lives and believes in me will never die.'

She-li This teacher talks in riddles.

Martha And then he asked me if I believed this. I said I did, because I just knew that I could trust him whatever he said, because he's the Messiah, you see, the one God promised would come into the world. And then he asked for Mary, so I ran back to the house and got her. You tell them the rest, Mary.

(During the following speeches Martha busies herself taking down the washing, then settles down on the ground in front of the house.)

Mary Yes, Martha. I wrote it down in my diary as well. *(Referring to notes, fairly subdued to begin with, but gradually getting more excited.)* So I hurried off down the road to meet him, and all the people in the house who were there to comfort me followed on behind. I think they thought I was going to the grave to weep there.

She-li Ah, yes, the grave. We're glad you mentioned that ...

Mary When I saw Jesus I just fell on the ground in front of him and wept. I kept saying over and over again, 'If only you had been here, Lord. If only you had been here.' And everyone was crying and wailing, it was an awful scene. And you could tell that Jesus was deeply moved by it all. He asked me where we'd buried him, so we told him to come and see. And when we got there he just stood in front of the tomb ... and he wept as well. And everyone was saying how much he must have loved our brother.

Eli I do not understand. If this healer loved him so much, why did he not save him from dying?

Mary Just let me tell you what happened, will you?

She-li Just let her tell you what happened, will you, brother?

Mary Well, you remember the tomb—it was a sort of cave with a large stone placed in front to seal it, right?

She-li We remember it well.

Eli Single tomb, grade two, no extras. Two hundred and twenty shekels.

Mary Well, Jesus went up to it and ordered the stone to be taken away.

She-li But your brother had been dead for four days. The smell!

Martha That's what I said. But Jesus told us that we would see the glory of God if we just believed!

Mary And they took the stone away and Jesus looked up to heaven and prayed *(reads notes carefully)*: 'I thank you, Father, that you listen to me. I know you always listen to me, but I say this for the sake of the people here, so that they will believe that you sent me.' And then he called out in a loud voice, 'Lazarus, come out!'

Eli This is a strange way of comforting two grieving sisters.

(During the final speech, Mary gives up on the two undertakers and goes across to join Martha on the ground outside the house.)

She-li Huh, Lazarus, come out! *(Finding this very amusing.)* That is a good one. I like that. Lazarus, come out. *(Mockingly, as though calling towards the tomb, away from the house.)* Lazarus, yoo-hoo, Lazarus, come out . . . *(Eli gradually joins in with the fun.)* Lazarus, where are you? Lazarus, come out now.

(Lazarus suddenly pops his head out of the window of the house.)

Lazarus You called?

(Eli and She-li turn and react with astonishment. She-li faints, Eli fans She-li with the copy of the accounts which he is holding. Lazarus comes out of the house, Mary and Martha get up, he takes their arms and they begin to walk off, stopping as they pass the undertakers.)

Martha Didn't you listen to what we told you? What the Lord Jesus said?

Mary I am the resurrection and the life.

Martha Whoever believes in me will live . . .

Lazarus . . . even though he dies.

(They walk off, Mary handing Eli his payment as she goes. She-li comes round. Eli and She-li get up and begin to walk off.)

Eli What do you think, She-li? Could there be a future in the secondhand trade? *(Exit.)*

THE LORD LOOKS AT THE HEART

Bible Base: 1 Samuel 16.1–13.

Introduction: This simple sketch, based on the story of Samuel anointing David as King of Israel, provides an opportunity for all the available children to participate in an enjoyable piece of drama. The message is straightforward and direct, and cannot be put more effectively than was done by the prophet Samuel himself: 'Man looks at the outward appearance, but the Lord looks at the heart.' Much of the impact of the sketch arises from the use of repetition, as, one after the other, the sons of Jesse are rejected. The Chorus should practise making the repeated sequence very rhythmical.

Cast: The prophet Samuel, Jesse, David, six other sons, one daughter, the Chorus.

(All available children, except for Jesse, Samuel and David, form a Chorus, arranged in a semi-circle facing the audience. Samuel enters from one side and addresses the audience.)

Samuel I am Samuel, the prophet. Only a small prophet, but blame the recession. The Lord has sent me to Bethlehem, to the home of Jesse. *(Jesse enters from the other side and stands at the opposite corner to Samuel.)* He has chosen one of Jesse's sons to be the next King of Israel.

Chorus *(whisper, in a 'wow' voice)* The next King of Israel!

Samuel *(to Jesse)* The Lord has sent me to anoint one of your sons as the next King of Israel.

Chorus *(louder)* The next King of Israel!

Jesse *(calling out)* Step forward, number one son. *(Number one son steps forward from the Chorus: for extra humour use a short child for this part.)* Is this the one chosen? *(Pointing at the son.)* Is this the next King of Israel?

Chorus The next King of Israel?

Jesse Look at this fine young man. Just what you'd want for a king. Handsome, strong—and very tall. *(Number one son gets up on a box.)*

Chorus *(raising their hands to indicate height)* Look at all those centimetres!

Jesse Surely, he's the one!

Chorus *(to Samuel, pointing to son)* Is he the one?

Samuel Well . . .

Chorus Yes?

Samuel Perhaps . . .

Chorus *(louder)* Yes?

Samuel Maybe . . .

Chorus *(louder and higher)* Yes?

Samuel No!

Chorus No?

Samuel No!

Chorus *(disappointed)* Oh!

> *(Number one son returns to Chorus.)*

Jesse *(calling out)* Step forward, number two son. *(Number two son steps forward from the Chorus: he gets out his wallet and starts counting £5 notes.)* Is this the one chosen? *(Pointing at the son.)* Is this the next King of Israel?

Chorus The next King of Israel?

Jesse This one's a successful businessman. Rich, ambitious, doing very nicely, thank you.

Chorus *(making an appropriate gesture to indicate lots of money)* Loads-a-shekels!

Jesse Surely, he's the one!

Chorus *(to Samuel, pointing to son)* Is he the one?

Samuel Well . . .

Chorus Yes?

Samuel Perhaps . . .

Chorus *(louder)* Yes?

Samuel Maybe . . .

Chorus *(louder and higher)* Yes?

Samuel No!

Chorus No?

Samuel No!

Chorus *(disappointed)* Oh!

> *(Number two son returns to Chorus.)*

Jesse *(calling out)* Step forward, number three son. *(Number three son steps forward from the Chorus: he should be dressed in trendy clothes, including jeans.)* Is this the one chosen? *(Pointing at the son.)* Is this the next King of Israel?

Chorus The next King of Israel?

Jesse Now he's a really trendy dresser. Look at the clothes, Samuel! Impressive!

Chorus Dig those Levis, Sammy-baby!

Jesse Surely, he's the one!

Chorus *(to Samuel, pointing to son)* Is he the one?

Samuel Well . . .

Chorus Yes?

Samuel Perhaps . . .

Chorus *(louder)* Yes?

Samuel Maybe . . .

Chorus *(louder and higher)* Yes?

Samuel No!

Chorus No?

Samuel No!

Chorus *(disappointed)* Oh!

> *(Number three son returns to Chorus.)*

Jesse *(calling out)* Step forward, number four son. *(Number four son steps forward from the Chorus: he is dressed in a football strip.)* Is this the one chosen? *(Pointing at the son.)* Is this the next King of Israel?

Chorus The next King of Israel?

Jesse How about a sportsman for a king? The best goalie we've ever had. *(Someone throws a football from the front row of the audience; number four son saves it.)*

Chorus What a save!

Jesse Surely, he's the one!

Chorus *(to Samuel, pointing to son)* Is he the one?

Samuel Well . . .

Chorus Yes?

Samuel Perhaps . . .

Chorus *(louder)* Yes?

Samuel Maybe . . .

Chorus *(louder and higher)* Yes?

Samuel No!

Chorus No?

Samuel No!

Chorus *(disappointed)* Oh!

    (Number four son returns to Chorus.)

Jesse *(calling out, but beginning to sound rather fed up with the whole business)* Step forward, number five son. *(Number five son steps forward from the Chorus.)* Is this the one chosen? *(Pointing at the son.)* Is this the next King of Israel?

Chorus The next King of Israel?

Jesse Now this is the brains of the family! Knows his 7-times table backwards.

Samuel What's seven times five then?

Number Five Son Fifty-three.

Chorus See what we mean?

Jesse Surely, he's the one!

Chorus *(to Samuel, pointing to son)* Is he the one?

Samuel Well ...

Chorus Yes?

Samuel Perhaps ...

Chorus *(louder)* Yes?

Samuel Maybe ...

Chorus *(louder and higher)* Yes?

Samuel No!

Chorus No?

Samuel No!

Chorus *(disappointed)* Oh!

    (Number five son returns to Chorus.)

Jesse *(beginning to sound desperate)* Step forward, number six son. *(Number six son steps forward from the Chorus: he is carrying a 'doctored' telephone directory.)* Is this the one chosen? *(Pointing at the son.)* Is this the next King of Israel?

Chorus The next King of Israel?

Jesse Now, he's the strong one in the family. Go on, muscles, show him your party trick. *(Number six son tears the telephone directory in half. Chorus cheer and clap; he takes a bow.)*

Jesse Surely, he's the one!

Chorus *(to Samuel, pointing to son)* Is he the one?

Samuel Well . . .

Chorus Yes?

Samuel Perhaps . . .

Chorus *(louder)* Yes?

Samuel Maybe . . .

Chorus *(louder and higher)* Yes?

Samuel No!

Chorus No?

Samuel No!

Chorus *(disappointed)* Oh!

> *(Number six son returns to Chorus.)*

Jesse *(optimistic again)* Step forward, number one daughter! *(Number one daughter steps forward from the Chorus.)* Is this the one chosen? *(Pointing at the daughter.)* Is this the next King of Israel?

Chorus The next King of Israel?

Samuel A girl?

Chorus Equal opportunities!

Jesse Surely, she's the one!

Chorus *(to Samuel, pointing to daughter)* Is she the one?

Samuel Well . . .

Chorus Yes?

Samuel Perhaps . . .

Chorus *(louder)* Yes?

Samuel Maybe . . .

Chorus *(louder and higher)* Yes?

Samuel No!

Chorus No?

Samuel No!

Chorus *(disappointed)* Oh!

> *(Number one daughter returns to Chorus.)*

Samuel Are there any more? *(Jesse counts the children . . .)*

Jesse Well, there is David. He's the youngest in the family. He's looking after the sheep.

Chorus David! *(They fall about laughing.)*

Samuel Quiet! Bring David here. *(Jesse goes to fetch him.)* Remember this: we look at the outward appearance, but the Lord looks at a person's heart. *(Jesse returns with David.)* Is this David?

Jesse This is David.

Chorus *(with disbelief)* Is he the one?

Samuel *(pause)* Yes. He is the one!

Chorus No!

Samuel Yes!

Chorus No!

Samuel Yes! David, I anoint you as the next King of Israel. *(Appropriate action.)*

Chorus *(kneeling)* The next King of Israel.

THE GIRL FROM MOAB

Bible Base: Ruth, chapters 1 and 2.

Introduction: This is a serious piece of drama dealing with the choice of Ruth to align herself with the people of God. It is hoped to challenge the audience to consider whether they too would be prepared to make personal sacrifices in being associated with the Lord's people.

Cast: Ruth, Boaz, Simon (Boaz's foreman), Orpah, Naomi, Narrator.

(The actors will need simple middle-eastern costumes. One part of the stage should be strewn with straw to represent the field in which Ruth is gleaning. Ruth enters, gleaning. Boaz and Simon enter, conversing, and take up a position at one corner of the stage.)

Boaz Well, Simon, how is the harvesting coming along?

Simon Very well, master. Once again the Lord is to be thanked for blessing the fields of Boaz with a rich harvest.

Boaz And a rich harvest for the gleaners as well, eh? *(He gestures towards Ruth.)* Tell me, Simon, who is that young woman working over there? Is she a foreigner?

Simon Ah, yes, that is the Moabite woman, Ruth. She came back from Moab recently with your kinswoman Naomi. I gave her permission to gather some gleanings behind the harvesters. Shall I send her away?

Boaz No, let her stay.

Simon She's a hard worker, that one. Here at the crack of dawn and working solidly all day with hardly a break.

(Ruth exits slowly with her bundle of straw.)

Boaz It sounds as though she could teach some of our Hebrew women a thing or two!

Simon True. And they say she has a character to match her beauty.

Boaz *(looking in the direction in which Ruth has departed)* If that is so then she must be truly an exceptional person. Tell me more, Simon, for I am greatly intrigued by this young foreigner who comes gleaning in my fields.

(They walk across to the other side of the stage as they converse.)

Simon You remember your kinsman Elimelech, Naomi's husband, and their two sons, who left Bethlehem during the great drought.

Boaz Yes . . .

Simon They settled for some time in Moab, and after Elimelech had died the two boys married Moabite women. Ruth was one of them.

Boaz But did not the two boys die very soon after their father?

Simon That's right. A terrible tragedy. Three widows in one household. *(Enter Naomi, Ruth and Orpah from the opposite side of the stage.)* Poor old Naomi decided eventually to return to her home here in Bethlehem to be with the people of God.

(Boaz and Simon exit.)

Naomi *(turning to Orpah and Ruth)* My daughters, I am determined to return to my own home, the town of Bethlehem in the land of Judah. You have been very kind to me as you were to my sons when they were alive. But now they are dead you are released from any obligation to stay with me. Go back each of you to your own mother's home, and may the Lord grant that you will find rest in the home of another husband.

Ruth No, Naomi. We will go back with you to your people.

Naomi Return home, my daughters. There is no future for you with me. I am an old woman now. Go back to your own people, and I will return to mine.

(They embrace, weeping. Orpah says farewell, and leaves. Ruth clings to Naomi.)

Naomi Look, Ruth. Orpah your sister is returning to her people and to her gods. Will you not do the same? You do not have to stay with me any longer.

Ruth Dear Naomi, do not urge me any more to leave you. Where you go I will go. Where you stay I will stay. Your people will be my people. And your God will be my God. Where you die I will die, and there I will be buried. I promise you before the Lord our God that nothing but death will now separate you and me.

Naomi Oh, Ruth, my dear, dear Ruth.

(They embrace and exit. Boaz and Simon re-enter and take up their earlier positions.)

Boaz I want you to take special care of this woman Ruth, Simon. See that she is not pestered by any of the men. I must confess that I feel drawn towards her.

Simon I will see to it, Boaz. You are swayed by the beauty of this foreigner, I fear?

Boaz Not just her beauty, Simon.

Simon *(laughing)* Oh yes, it would be a strange Jew who did not find attractive a woman who works as hard as that one!

Boaz That is true! Both her beauty and her diligence are indeed great treasures. *(Simon exits. Boaz speaks to himself.)* But what I treasure most is that when she was faced with the choice of returning to the comfort and security of her own kind or risking an unknown future here, she chose to align herself with the Lord's people. To find such courage and loyalty to the people of God in a foreign girl gleaning in my fields–Boaz, my man, I believe you have opened your purse looking for a shekel and found it full of gold pieces!

(Ruth re-enters, gleaning, as at the start of the play. Boaz approaches her.)

Boaz Ruth.

(She looks startled and fearful.)

Boaz Do not be frightened. I am happy for you to glean in my fields. Stay here with my servant girls and you will be safe. And if you are thirsty, go and get a drink from the water jars the men have filled over there. My foreman will look after you.

Ruth But, master Boaz, I am just a foreign girl. Why have I found such favour in your eyes?

Boaz I have been told all about what you have done for your mother-in-law since the death of your husband. How you left your father and mother and your homeland and came to live with a people you did not know before. Because you have chosen to join yourself to the people of God your faith and loyalty should be rewarded. Not just by me. But by the Lord, the God of Israel, under whose wing you have come to take refuge.

(They freeze. The Narrator enters and reads from a scroll.)

Narrator So Boaz took Ruth and she became his wife. And the Lord enabled her to conceive and she gave birth to a son. And they named him Obed. Obed was the father of Jesse. And Jesse was the father of David, who became the King of Israel. And from the descendants of King David was born Jesus, the Christ, the Saviour of the world.

WHO'S AT THE DOOR?

Bible Base: Revelation 3.20.

Introduction: This is a little modern-day domestic scene based on the image which Christ used in the message to the church in Laodicea: 'I stand at the door and knock. If anyone hears my voice and opens the door, I will go in and eat with him, and he with me.'

Cast: George and Fiona Carruthers, and their daughter. Voice off-stage.

(George and Fiona, a rather self-satisfied middle-class couple, are sitting in front of a television. George is reading a newspaper, and Fiona a magazine.)

Fiona What's on the box tonight, George darling?

George A vase of flowers and the *TV Times* by the look of it.

Fiona *(sarcastic)* Oh George, darling, you're so witty. With a mind like yours for company, who needs television, I ask myself.

George With programmes like these, who needs television? Look at it —repeats, old films, crummy situation comedies. Once *Neighbours* is over there's nothing worth watching for the rest of the evening. *(There is a knock at the door.)* It's hardly worth paying the licence fee.

Fiona George, darling, you haven't paid the licence fee for years.
(Knock at the door.)

George See who that is, Fiona, will you? *(Fiona goes to the door.)* I don't know, you just settle down to watch a bit of telly ... *(Fiona opens the door and has an imaginary conversation. George operates the remote control module.)* I don't suppose there's anything worth watching on Channel 4? No, I thought not.

Fiona *(calling)* George, darling, there's a woman here, wants to know if we're interested in double glazing.

George Tell her to get lost.

Fiona My husband says 'no, thank you'. *(Fiona closes the door, and returns.)*

George I'm fed up with these salesmen ...

Fiona Salespersons, George ...

George Well, whatever they are, coming round here, interrupting our evening's viewing . . . here, pass me that felt tip thingy, I've got an idea. This'll put a stop to it. *(Fiona passes him a felt tip pen. He writes on a sheet of card.)* 'To all salesmen'–sorry–'salespersons . . . do not bother to knock. This is a fully equipped house. We are watching telly and do not wish to be disturbed.'

Fiona *(sarcastic)* Beautifully put, George, poetry.

(George gets up and goes across to the door, opens it and attaches the notice on the outside.)

George Right, that's telling them.

(They settle down. There is another knock. George explodes!)

Fiona Now calm down, George. You take one of your tablets. I'll see who it is. *(She goes to the door. Appropriate action as she converses with the imaginary caller.)* They're collecting for 'Help the Aged', George.

George Tell them we gave them Granny last year.

Fiona *(ignores this)* Look, here's ten pence. See what you can do with that.

George Ask for a receipt.

(Fiona closes the door, returns.)

Fiona George, you really are impossible at times.

George I just get fed up with all these people intruding on my life. Why can't they just leave us alone? *(He starts to write another notice.)*

Fiona Now what are you writing?

George There. 'Charity collectors. Do not bother to knock. The residents here are mean, stingy, selfish, and also broke, on account of having spent all their readies on fully equipping this house–see above notice–we have nothing left to give you. Please leave us in peace.'

(He goes across and fixes the notice on the door. Returns, and they settle down.)

Fiona Something interesting on Channel 4, George? *(George is absorbed in the television now and ignores her.)* Cup of tea, darling? Two spoonfuls of arsenic as usual? I hear there's been an earthquake in Potters Bar, fifty thousand yuppies feared dead.

(Loud knock. Fiona looks nervous. George gets up without saying a word and, without taking his eyes off the TV, walks across to the door, opens it, pauses, slams it, returns to his seat and writes another notice.)

George 'Door-to-door evangelists, Mormons, JWs, Anglicans, we do not wish to be saved today, thank you. We are a lost cause. We are quite content to spend our lives watching our 28 inch flat-screen colour TV, and get very unpleasant if interrupted.' *(Goes and fixes this notice. Returns, settles down.)* Now I've missed the end of that programme I was watching.

Fiona Shall I make a cup of tea, darling? *(Yet another knock. George reacts.)* You stay there, George, I'll deal with them. *(She rushes to the door. Appropriate action, then she calls across to George.)* It's our local Labour Party candidate. He wants to know if he can rely on our vote?

George Tell him . . .

Fiona It's all right, George, I've already told him. *(Closes the door.)*

George I've had enough of this, Fiona. It's just one after the other. Who will it be next? Look, take down those notices . . . I'll do another one . . . *(appropriate action)* . . . 'Whoever you are: do not bother to knock on this door. You have nothing that we want; we have nothing to give you; we are quite content as we are; please leave us alone; just stay out of our lives. Thank you. George and Fiona Carruthers, the residents.'

(Fiona takes this and puts it up on the door. She returns and makes a cup of tea . . . they settle down. There is a gentle knock at the door. George and Fiona look at each other.)

Fiona No, George, I don't think it was a knock.

(Louder knocking: they look at each other.)

George It must be the representative of the National Society of Non-readers.

Fiona Just ignore it, George. They'll go away eventually.

(Louder knocking: George puts on headphones, Fiona carefully places cotton-wool in her ears. The knocking goes on . . .)

Voice *(outside)* Hello . . . is anybody there . . . hello? Can you hear me? . . . *(knocking)* If you can hear me, will you open the door please? . . . Hello? George? Fiona? Will you let me in? *(knocking)* You only have to open the door. Hello? Are you in there? *(George and Fiona drop off to sleep. The knocking and calling become fainter. The lights go down. The knocking and calling stop. After a while the lights come up. There is the sound of a key turning in the door. Daughter enters cheerfully, picking up a card from the doormat as she does so. She's singing the theme tune of 'Neighbours' to herself, as she busies herself clearing up the cups and papers. George and Fiona are motionless.)*

Daughter Oh, hello, Mum and Dad. Just called in to see how you are. Been watching telly all night again? Tut, tut, you'll go square-eyed, you know. Oh, by the way, there was this card for you on the doormat. *(Looks at card and reads)* 'To George and Fiona Carruthers. I stood at your door and knocked. I knocked time and time again. I called to you by name. If you had heard my voice and opened the door I would have come in. But now it is too late. I called and you did not answer.' I wonder who it was? Who do you think it was, Mum? . . . Dad? *(She goes across to them — there is a hint of panic in her voice.)* Mum! . . . Dad! *(They do not respond: blackout.)*

NOT BY WORKS

Bible Base: Romans 3.22–24; Romans 6.23; 1 John 1.8–9; Ephesians 2.8–9.

Introduction: This is a play in four scenes which explores the teaching of Ephesians 2.8–9: that we cannot earn our way to heaven by our own efforts. Salvation is 'not by works', but by grace. The first three scenes are based on three characters with common misconceptions about how to get to heaven. In scene 4, the characters re-appear on Judgement Day . . .

Cast: Daley Mark, an athlete (scenes 1 and 4), Stanley Bend, a plumber (scenes 2 and 4), Ivy May Perfect, an examination candidate (scenes 3 and 4), Ron Rabbiton, a sports commentator (scene 1), Clerk (scene 2), Examiner (scene 3), Receptionist (scene 4), Christian (scene 4). Since not all characters appear in all scenes, some actors may take more than one part.

(Replace local references appropriately to suit your own situation.)

SCENE ONE: A Target to Aim for?

Ron Rabbiton *(speaking into a hand mike)* Good evening, ladies and gentlemen, this is Ron Rabbiton welcoming you to the stage of Surrey Chapel, Norwich, where we are approaching what might be a historic moment in the life of this quaint little evangelical Free Church community. We are going to witness here tonight in this very building an attempt by one of the members of the congregation to break the Surrey Chapel all-comers' long jump record. And now here is the man himself–he's been in training for weeks for this attempt on the record and he reckons he's in the peak of condition–here he is, from the Mulbarton Athletics and Ballroom Dancing Club–Mr Daley Mark.

(Enter Daley from behind screen, on crutches with leg in plaster. Ron is somewhat taken aback by his condition.)

Ron Er, um, you're, er, going to attempt the long jump record?

Daley *(full of confidence)* Yes, of course. Why, what's the matter?

Ron *(obviously looking at the broken leg)* Oh, sure, fine. Of course, the long jump record. Um, you don't want to leave it for a week or two until . . . *(indicating the leg, but not wanting to mention it).*

Daley Until what?

Ron Oh nothing, I just thought . . .you're really in the peak of condition then?

Daley Never felt better.

Ron Right, well, we'd better get on with it. *(Daley Mark takes up his position ready to jump.)*

Ron *(speaking in an excited whisper)* So, here we are, then. Daley Mark is about to attempt to set a new Surrey Chapel all-comers' record for the long jump. The existing record, remember, is two feet seven and a half inches and was set by six-year-old David Gallop, on Sunday June 18th last year during the second hymn of the morning Family Service. OK, Mr Mark, it's all up to you now.

(Daley prepares himself and eventually, after an appropriate build-up, makes a suitably small hop across the stage. Ron gets the tape and measures distance.)

Daley *(excitedly)* Have I broken it?

Ron What? Your leg?

Daley No, the record!

Ron Oh, the record! Let's see . .that's two feet, and, yes, you've broken the record: two feet eight inches! Ladies and gentlemen, a new Surrey Chapel all-comers' long jump record! Remember you saw it here tonight on the . . . *(insert the current date).*

Daley *(interrupting)* So have I made it, then?

Ron Made what?

Daley Do I get in?

Ron In?

Daley Do I get in the team for the next Olympics? Have I reached the qualifying standard?

Ron Oh, I don't know about that. Let me see now. *(Looks through papers.)* No, I don't think so.

Daley But I've done better than anyone else in Surrey Chapel. What do I have to do to get into the squad for the next Olympics?

Ron You're not going to like this. Let's see, Mr Mark, you made it to about . . .here *(points to where he landed)* and, according to the rules, you'd have to jump to *(measures out an enormously long distance)* about . . .here *(points to a spot on the ground)* to reach the required standard. And, I think *(looking from one spot to the other)* you're just a little short of the target, wouldn't you say?

Daley *(stunned)* Well, I think that's ridiculous! No-one could reach that standard. Even without a broken leg! *(Throws away crutches and stomps off.)*

Ron Well, ladies and gentlemen, although a new record has been set here this evening, it seems that Mr Mark has still missed the mark. This is Ron Rabbiton on the stage at Surrey Chapel, Norwich, handing you back to the studio.

SCENE TWO: A Wage to be Earned?

(The Clerk is seated at a table. Stanley Bend, a plumber, enters to collect his wages. She doesn't look up. He coughs to attract her attention. She still ignores him.)

Stan Excuse me, miss, I've come for my wages, please.

Clerk *(without looking up)* Name and occupation?

Stan Stanley Bend, plumber. *(Points to one of the envelopes.)* Look, there it is: S. Bend.

Clerk Sign here. *(She hands him a sheet of paper; he signs it; she hands over the wages envelope, all this without looking up.)*

Stan Thank you! *(He opens the envelope as he walks away. It is empty. He's horrified, then thinks it's a joke.)* Ha, ha, very funny. April the first, is it? Now, can I have my wages, please?

Clerk Name and occupation?

Stan I've already told you. Stanley Bend, plumber. Now stop mucking about and give me my wages.

Clerk *(checking list)* Sorry, you've had them. This is your signature, I believe?

Stan But the envelope was empty. Look. I've done five days' solid work this week *(checking his book)*. I reckon you owe me, let's see, two hundred and eighty-five pounds, twenty-six pence. All I ask for is what I've earned. I've fixed four loos, changed fourteen washers, got rid of the leeks in the kitchen sink for that Welsh woman, and then did four hours overtime on Saturday morning fixing taps for that house in Clarendon Rd.

Clerk Oh, yes, we had a complaint about that. The owner rang to say that when he said 'tap on the kitchen door when you've finished' he didn't actually mean you to put a tap on the kitchen door.

Stan Well, I don't know about that. All I know is that you owe me £285.26.

Clerk That's right, Mr Bend, £285.26, for five days, plus four hours' overtime. Now that will be less income tax, national insurance, and pension fund, of course. Then we've had to deduct £75 for bodging that job in Clarendon Rd. And according to our records you were late for work Monday, knocked off early on Friday, and we've taken into account your exaggerated mileage claims over the last year, the firm's tools that have somehow managed to finish up in your toolbox at home, plus two packets of paper clips and no end of office stationery . . . *(Stan begins to look sheepish and gradually edges off-stage)* . . . plus one or two other minor misdemeanours over the past year which have caused the firm a certain amount of embarrassment and financial disadvantage. So, all in all, we reckon that what you have earned is, well, let's put it this way, you actually owe us, let's see *(checking papers)*, one hundred and three pounds, seventeen pence. Call it a round hundred. But you needn't settle it now. We can deduct it from next month's . . . *(looks up and sees that Stan has gone)*. Oh, he's gone. Oh, well. Never mind. It's funny, though, he seemed a bit surprised. He did ask for what he had earned. And, after all, that was exactly what we'd given him. *(Packs up papers and exits.)*

SCENE THREE: An Exam to be Passed?

(Ivy is seated at a desk. The Examiner is sitting facing her, as though invigilating.)

Examiner Name?

Ivy Ivy May Perfect, Miss.

Examiner Name on the paper, please.

Ivy Right. *(Writes)* Name . . . I. M. Perfect.

Examiner Right, quiet please, the examination is about to begin. This GCSE in Personal Religion is a two-hour paper. You must answer every question. Do not attempt to write on both sides of the paper at the same time. You may now begin. *(Examiner walks up and down invigilating.)*

Ivy *(talking to herself)* Right. Here goes. Question 1. Are you a Christian? *(Writes answer.)* 'Yes, of course I am.' Huh, what do they think I am? Question 2. What does it mean to be a Christian? Now let's think. *(Writes)* 'Go to church . . . live a moral life . . . traditional Christian values . . . live in a Christian country . . .' Question 3. What are your own personal values? Easy. 'I believe it is important to be honest and straightforward, to respect other people, to care for your family, and to be kind to those less fortunate than myself.' In other words, traditional Christian values. Question 4. How does your own life measure up to God's standards? Mm, tricky, that one. Could be a catch here. But I don't know, though, I don't do too badly. Let's have a go at it. *(Writes)* 'I think of myself as basically a decent, hard-working, honest sort of a person. I look after my family. I don't steal. I give money to charity. I'm always kind to old people and animals. I keep my home clean and tidy.' Not like some people I could name. 'I've got a clean driving licence, never get drunk, I don't smoke and I certainly don't go round annoying people with one of those confounded ghetto-blasters. To sum up: I suppose I may have my faults, like most people, but basically, I've done nothing to be ashamed of.' Right, I think that should be enough to impress the examiners. On to Question 5. Are you guilty of any of the following: pride, complacency, selfishness, arrogance, deceit? Mm. 'No.' That was an easy one. Now Question 6. Do you expect to pass this examination? 'Yes.'

Examiner Right, time's up. Stop writing. Make sure your name is on your paper. Leave your paper on the desk when you go. Thank you.

(Ivy leaves. Examiner picks up script. Sits and marks it. Ivy re-enters.)

Ivy How've I done then? Have I passed? I found it dead easy really. I wouldn't be surprised if I got all the questions right.

(Examiner shakes her head and hands over the script. Ivy is aghast, and walks off shocked.)

Examiner *(as she goes)* I told her time and time again to read the paper carefully. But she wouldn't listen.

SCENE FOUR: Judgement Day

(Daley, Stan, Ivy and Christian sit on a bench as in a waiting room, reading. Christian is left out of the conversation, but, thoughtfully, observes what is going on. There is a screen in one corner of the stage.)

Daley *(discarding a copy of an appropriate magazine, such as the church magazine)* You'd think they'd get some decent magazines in this waiting room, wouldn't you?

Ivy Don't get all ratty now. Just because you're worried about what he's going to say.

Daley Worried? Who, me? I've got nothing to worry about. I've done my best, haven't I?

Stan So, what are you going to say when you get in there, then?

Daley I don't know, really. But I'm pretty confident. I've lived a good life. I've done a lot better than most people I can think of.

Stan You sure?

Daley Well, come on then. Tell me who's lived a better life than I have?

Ivy How about the Archbishop of Canterbury?

Stan Jimmy Savile.

Ivy Mother Teresa.

Stan Margaret Thatcher.

Daley Don't be stupid. I'm talking about ordinary people like you and me.

Ivy Jesus? He was just an ordinary person . . .

Daley Yes, sure, but he didn't have to put up with people like you lot, did he? Anyway, I think of it rather like a long jumper aiming for a target. You set your sights on reaching a certain sort of standard in life and you go for it.

Ivy And you reckon you've reached it?

Stan I know what you mean, Daley. I think of it like working for a fair wage. You work hard, put in the hours and then you get what you deserve.

Ivy So you reckon you've earned your entrance fee, then?

Stan Well, I must get some credit for what I've done. I feel fairly confident I've notched up a few points over the years. I've lived a decent sort of a life, helped other people when I can . . .

Receptionist *(appearing from behind the screen)* He's ready to see you now, Mr Mark. Would you like to go in, please?

Daley OK then. Here goes. See you inside, folks. *(Daley gets up, and the Receptionist escorts him behind the screen.)*

Ivy Do you think he'll be OK?

Stan I should think so. He seems fairly confident. What about you?

Ivy Oh, I'm sure I'll pass all right. I think I know all the right answers. I've been through my life and honestly I can't see anything wrong really. I suppose I may have one or two little faults, but I'm basically decent and honest at heart. Respect for other people, that's what counts, doesn't it? You get a lot of marks for that, I reckon.

(Daley re-enters from behind the screen, looking at a card. He is clearly distraught, and walks past the others as they talk to him, eventually discarding the card as he leaves the stage.

Stan Oh, Daley, you're back.

Ivy How'd you get on?

Stan Did you . . . make it? You reached the target?

Daley It's ridiculous. No-one could live up to those standards. *(Exit Daley. Ivy picks up the card and reads it.)*

Stan What does it say?

Ivy It says: Have you not read what is written in the word of God? There is no difference. All have sinned and fall short . . . and fall short . . . of the glory of God.

Receptionist *(appearing from behind the screen again)* Next please. Mr Bend, I think you're next.

Stan OK, see you inside, Miss. I'm off to collect my wages, if you get my meaning. *(Stands up. Receptionist takes him behind the screen.)*

Ivy And then there was one. *(She idly reads the card left by Daley.)* 'There is no difference . . . all have sinned and fall short . . .'
(Stan comes back from behind the screen, reading a card, looking rather sheepish.)

Ivy Oh, back already, Mr Bend? *(Stan walks off, discarding his card. Ivy picks it up, and reads it.)* 'Have you not read what is written in the word of God: For the wages of sin . . . the wages of sin . . . is death.' Oh, no. I don't believe it. He thought he'd earned eternal life, and . . . now . . .
(Receptionist enters again.)

Receptionist Your turn, Miss Perfect.

Ivy *(rather unsure now)* Right. OK. Well, here goes then. Nothing to worry about, Ivy. You know all the answers. You'll pass all right. Full marks for a decent life.
(She goes behind screen, leaving Stan's card on the bench. The Receptionist picks it up and calls out after her, but too late.)

Receptionist Wait a bit, didn't you read the rest of this? . . . Too late. *(Turns towards Christian.)* She never would listen. Never read the paper properly when she was at school. If only once in her life she had stopped and read what God's word actually says . . . *(Ivy returns, studying a card, looking shaken.)* Oh, Miss Perfect, you're back already. Look, didn't you see what it said after the bit about the wages? . . . Look: 'the gift of God is eternal life in Christ Jesus our Lord.'

Ivy I failed. Failed abysmally. Look at this report: 'If we claim to be without sin, we deceive ourselves and the truth is not in us . . .' That's what he thinks of me. Deceiving myself. That's his verdict on Ivy May Perfect . . . *(Exits, handing card to Receptionist.)*

Receptionist *(looks at card)* I might have guessed it . . . only half the story, as usual. If only she'd paid attention to this when she had the chance. *(To Christian)* If only they all had. Oh, well, it's too late now, I'm afraid. *(Reads)* 'If we claim to be without sin, we deceive ourselves, and the truth is not in us. But if we confess our sins . . .

Christian . . . if we confess our sins, he is faithful and just, and will forgive us our sins and purify us from all unrighteousness.'

Receptionist That's right!

Christian Yes, and it's true, as well. Is it all right if I go in now?

Receptionist Oh, yes, of course. Sorry to keep you waiting. Oh, I'll take that, thank you. *(Christian hands over a card that he has been holding. The Receptionist looks at it, as Christian makes his way off behind the screen.)* Yes, that's fine. You go ahead. He's waiting for you. *(Reads)* 'It is not by works. It is by grace you have been saved, through faith. And this not from yourselves. *(Looks towards the screen.)* It is the gift of God.' *(Exits behind the screen.)*

THE LEAST OF THESE

Bible Base: Matthew 25.34–45.

Introduction: This play can be used and adapted for any occasion which is focusing on the challenge to support relief work world-wide, particularly work for the world's children. It was actually written for the TEAR Fund (The Evangelical Alliance Relief Fund) 'Weekend for the World's Children', and some reference to this has been left in the script, but with minor modifications it could well be used to support the work of other charities and organisations committed to helping children in need.

Cast: John, Sue, his wife, Pat, his sister, Voice off-stage, about a dozen children.

(John is seated at a table, preoccupied with some work. He occasionally looks up and joins in with the conversation, but he's not really interested. Sue, his wife, and Pat, his sister, are seated away from him. Pat is looking at some literature related to relief work for children in need world-wide. Sue is reading a magazine.)

Pat I see that TEAR Fund is calling this the 'Weekend for the World's Children'.

Sue Oh, that explains it. They've got a special service at the local church this morning.

Pat You going?

Sue Shouldn't think so. John's got his work to do. *(Shouts)* John, you want to go to church this morning? It's a special weekend for the world's children. TEAR Fund's organising it.

John *(doesn't look up)* Never heard of them.

Pat Never heard of what, John? Weekends? Or children?

John Make me a cup of coffee, Sue, will you. And while you're about it make one for my sister. It might shut her up for a while.

Sue *(mocking)* Yes, sir, right away, sir. Will there be anything else, sir? *(Exit.)*

Pat *(reading)* 'The rights of a child—the right to survival, the right to protection, the right to development.'

John And the rights of a working man—the right to a bit of peace and quiet in his own home at the weekend. *(Returns to his work.)* Sue, where did I put the calculator?

(Sue returns with coffee, puts it down somewhat aggressively on the table, walks across the room, finds the calculator and does the same with that. She returns to her seat.)

Pat *(consulting the literature, to Sue)* It says here that although nine babies in every thousand in Britain die before their first birthday, in Nepal it's 130 in every thousand, in Ethiopia 155 and in Mozambique, it's 170!

Sue A hundred and seventy babies in every thousand. That's awful.

Pat There are 25 million kids in Latin America suffering from malnutrition, even though the region is one of the world's major food exporters. Two hundred thousand children go blind very year because they don't get enough Vitamin A. Ten million cases of malnutrition and diarrhoea a year in babies because mothers who should be breast-feeding use contaminated water to prepare powdered milk.

John *(momentarily looking up from his work)* You can't do anything about it, Pat. Children are dying all round the world all the time.

Pat But you can! Listen: one of the biggest killers is diarrhoea—and it only costs 7p a dose to provide a simple sugar and salt drink which prevents children with diarrhoea dying from dehydration.

Sue It's called ORT, isn't it? Oral something-or-other treatment.

Pat Rehydration. Oral rehydration treatment. And, look *(handing Sue the literature)*, there's this clinic in Bangladesh, for example, supported by gifts from Christians in Britain. It's especially for the under-fives. And they don't just treat the children's illnesses, they immunise them and give the mothers training in health care and hygiene.

Sue *(leafing through the literature)* There seem to be dozens of projects like that all round the world—I suppose every little helps.

John *(muttering)* A little peace and quiet would help. *(Picking up a newspaper.)* Oh no, I don't believe it. The bank is putting up interest rates again. Another 1 per cent. So much for our plans for a loan for a new car.

Sue *(looking at John)* A little increase in interest wouldn't go amiss, if you ask me.

Pat Do you see those figures there about the ways in which children suffer at the hands of adults? It's horrifying.

Sue 'Nearly ten thousand children detained in prison in South Africa in the last three years. 150,000 babies in Africa infected with the AIDS virus.'

John Are you two trying to put me off my lunch?

Sue '20,000 children are being sexually exploited in the Philippines. Every three and a half minutes a child is killed by a war in Africa. 150 million of the world's children under the age of 15 have to work full-time.' These statistics are horrific.

Pat It makes you want to weep.

Sue Listen, Pat, this is incredible—three million children a year die from just six killer diseases. Any idea what they are?

Pat I should think it'll be tropical diseases like malaria? Cholera? Typhoid?

Sue No, in fact, they're just the sort of diseases which used to be quite common in Britain: polio, tetanus, measles, diphtheria, whooping cough and TB. They've just about disappeared in Britain because of vaccination—and it would only cost six hundred million pounds to wipe them out world-wide.

John Six hundred million pounds: that's serious money, Sue.

Sue Depends what you compare it with. They say here it's about the same as the cost of twenty military planes!

Pat I don't know, the world seems to have its values all upside down sometimes.

John Look, you two, there's no point in getting het up about it. You can't solve all the problems in the world. So relax, forget about it, enjoy what you've got. That's my philosophy.

Sue I still think we should try. Come on, Pat. Let's go along to this church service and see what gives.

Pat OK. You sure you don't want to come, John?

John No, thanks. I've got to get this pile of work done by nine o'clock Monday morning, otherwise the boss'll be talking redundancy again.

Sue Well, see if you can find a few minutes to look at this while we're gone.

(Sue hands John the literature. They leave. John does a little more work on his papers, then picks up the literature and reads it. 'The voice of God' is heard over a loudspeaker. At the same time a procession of children enters from the back of the hall. They represent the deprived, suffering and abused children of the world— in rags, bandages, chains, blind, holding begging bowls, carrying heavy implements, buckets, etc. They process up the

aisle on to the stage, passing John, who does not see them, off stage and to their seats. They mutter quietly phrases like 'help me', 'I want some water', 'give me some food', 'free me' . . . The procession should be timed so that the last child passes John as the Voice completes the second speech.)

John *(reading)* Then the King will say to those on his left . . .

Voice Depart from me, you who are cursed. For I was hungry and you gave me nothing to eat. I was thirsty and you gave me nothing to drink. I was a stranger and you did not invite me in. I needed clothes and you did not clothe me. I was sick and in prison and you did not look after me.

John *(standing and reacting angrily)* Now hold on a minute, Lord. When did I see you hungry? When did I see you thirsty? When did I see you a stranger, or needing clothes or sick or in prison—and did not help you? Now, come on, be fair.

Voice I tell you the truth. Whatever you did not do for one of the least of these, you did not do for me.

(John momentarily looks in the direction of the line of children, which has now passed him by. He sits and buries his head in his hands. Blackout.)

ODD ONE IN

Introduction: Here are four simple scripts, each based on passages in the Gospels, which show that Jesus had time for those who were excluded by others. They are designed for 'instant drama' with a group of children, for teaching and discussion rather than performance in the first instance. One effective way of handling them is to divide the children into four groups, each with an adult leader, and send them off into separate areas for ten minutes to prepare their scene. They then return and perform their scene to the other three groups, improvising action while the adult narrates the story. No suggestions for improvised actions are made in the scripts, since it is expected that the groups will work these out themselves. The scripts are deliberately simple and to the point, they provide plenty of opportunities for miming, and can involve a good number of children. Particularly important is that the children should try in their miming to express strong emotions, such as disgust and amazement. After the four scenes have been performed, discuss with the children what the four scenes have in common and what they teach us. Could the children devise a fifth, modern-day story to make a similar point?

SCENE ONE: Neighbours?

Bible Base: Luke 10.30–37.

Cast: Traveller, Robbers, Priest, Levite, Samaritan, Donkey.

Script: A Jewish man was travelling one day on the road from Jerusalem to Jericho. It was a hot, sunny day. He sat down by some rocks and wiped his brow.

'Phew,' he said to himself, looking up at the sky, 'what a scorcher!' He took a welcome drink from his water bottle.

But this was a very dangerous place. As he sat there, peacefully enjoying his drink, a gang of evil, ugly and nasty robbers were creeping up behind him. Slowly they crawled towards the unsuspecting traveller. Suddenly they pounced! The man was knocked over, beaten up, and all his belongings taken. The robbers disappeared into the hills, leaving the poor man lying half-dead on the roadside.

49

A little while later, a fat priest came waddling along the road. He was rather nervous, because he knew this place was famous for robbers. He saw the man lying on the roadside, groaning in agony. But did he stop to help?

(Everyone joins in with 'No'.) NO!

He just hurried by, on the other side of the road. He had business to attend to in Jerusalem.

Then a Levite came striding along. He saw the poor fellow lying on the roadside, stopped, and thought to himself what a disgrace it was that you couldn't travel the roads in safety these days. He tutted loudly. The man cried out, 'Help me! Help me! I'm dying!' But did the Levite help?

(Everyone) NO!

He also just hurried by, on the other side of the road.

A few minutes later, a Samaritan came along the road, with his faithful donkey at his side. Now Jews and Samaritans hated each other and normally would not even talk together. So when the Samaritan saw the Jewish man lying on the roadside, he wouldn't stop to help, would he?

(Everyone) YES!

He did! He went over to him, bandaged his wounds, poured on oil to soothe them, put the man on his donkey and took him to the nearest inn to be looked after.

SCENE TWO: Short Change

Bible Base: Luke 19.1–10.

Cast: Jesus, Crowd, Zacchaeus, the sycamore tree (probably an adult).

Script: Zacchaeus was a chief tax-collector. He was only a little chap, but he had loads-a-money—because the truth was that he was a crook. Everyone in Jericho hated him. When he walked down the road, they would all hiss and boo and turn their backs on him. Zacchaeus didn't have any friends. And quite frankly he didn't deserve them. He sat in his house, on his own and counted his money. A lonely man.

One day Jesus came into town on his way to Jerusalem. Everyone went out to see him. They crowded round Jesus and listened to his teaching as he walked along. Zacchaeus wanted to see who this Jesus was, but he was so small he couldn't see above the heads of the crowd. He ran round and round, jumping up and down, trying to see Jesus, but it was no good, and no-one would let him in.

Suddenly he had an idea. Just ahead of the crowd, a little way down the road, was a large sycamore tree. He ran as fast as his little legs would carry him and quickly climbed up the tree. From here he could see clearly—and there was Jesus, coming towards him now.

When Jesus reached the spot, he stopped. He looked up at the tree. So did all the crowd. They all laughed at the sight of the hated Zacchaeus, looking so stupid sitting up there in the branches. But to their surprise, Jesus spoke to the man. And spoke to him in a friendly way!

'Zacchaeus, come down immediately. I will stay at your house today.'

Zachaeus came down at once and took Jesus to his house. The crowd thought this was disgraceful.

'What is he doing? Going to eat in the house of a sinner, the house of that crook Zacchaeus! Huh! Disgraceful!'

And then Zacchaeus came back down the road. But this time he was not coming to collect money. He was giving it away! To every poor person he met he gave some money. And to everyone he had ever cheated he repaid four times the amount. And he invited them all to come to his house for a party to celebrate. And they all went, because Jesus had taught them that even someone like Zacchaeus needs and can respond to friendship and love.

SCENE THREE: An Unwelcome Guest

Bible Base: Luke 7.36–50.

Cast: Jesus, Simon the Pharisee, Guests, Mary.

Script: Simon was a rich and important man, a Pharisee. He had invited Jesus to dinner in his house to meet him and his friends. He welcomed his guests one by one and showed them to their seats around the table. They ate and drank well, and relaxed after the meal, while the Pharisee and his friends questioned Jesus about his teaching.

Meanwhile a young woman called Mary was creeping quietly through the dark streets towards the Pharisee's house. In her arms she carried a special, precious jar. Mary was not a very nice person. She had led a very wicked life and had got into all sorts of trouble. She was well-known around the town and no self-respecting person would be seen talking to her in public.

She crept up to the house and peeped in through the open window. Yes, there he was. Just as she had heard. The teacher, Jesus, the one she had seen doing miracles, the one she had heard teaching about forgiveness and the kingdom of heaven, the one whose teaching had so touched her own heart—there he was. This was her chance.

She burst in through the door, rushed into the room, threw herself at his feet and just burst into tears.

'Master, master!' she whispered. Jesus placed a hand on her head to reassure her. By now his feet were wet from her tears, and she wiped them dry with her hair, all the time whispering quietly, 'Master, master!

Help me!' The jar she carried was full of expensive perfume. And she opened it and just poured the whole lot on Jesus' feet—as a sign of her devotion.

Simon the Pharisee and his friends were furious! They tutted loudly, expressing their disapproval for the whole scene, and muttered things like 'shocking', 'disgraceful', 'disgusting'. Simon stood to his feet and pointed at Jesus.

'If this man really were a prophet,' he said to his friends, 'he would know what sort of woman this is that is touching him. A sinner! Ugh!'

Jesus silenced Simon. Did he not realise that it was because she was such a sinner that she loved him so much? Because he, Jesus, had brought her what she needed most of all.

He turned to Mary and just said quietly: 'Your sins are forgiven.'

Simon and all the other guests were stunned, and murmured amongst themselves: 'Who is this man who even forgives sins?'

Jesus said to Mary: 'Go in peace. Your faith has saved you.'

SCENE FOUR: Outcast

Bible Base: Matthew 8.1–4.

Cast: Jude, Jesus, Crowd.

Script: Jude suffered from a terrible skin disease. It made his hands and feet gradually rot away and turned him into a cripple. When the people in his village discovered that he had this disease, they drove him out of his home and made him live out in the countryside, away from his friends and family. Wherever he went he had to ring a bell and call out: 'Unclean, unclean!' so that people could keep well away from him. Because of his awful disease, Jude was an outcast.

One day Jesus came down the mountainside near to the village. A large crowd followed him. Jude saw him coming and knew at once this was the Jesus he had heard about, the one who could do miracles. He stumbled his way across the rough ground to where Jesus was. The people in the crowd saw him coming and stepped back in disgust. They didn't want to touch him and make themselves unclean. Jude fell on the ground in front of Jesus.

He looked up at Jesus and held out his diseased hands in despair: 'Lord, if you are willing, I know you can make me clean.'

Jesus reached out his hand—and touched the awful, rotting skin of the man in front of him. The crowd were amazed, disgusted, horrified—even angry. Touching an unclean leper. Ugh!

But Jesus looked at Jude, and loved him. 'I am willing,' he said. 'Be clean!'

An amazing surge of divine power shuddered through Jude's body. He stood up slowly and then looked at the skin on his hands. They were perfect again. All the dry, rotting skin was gone—he had hands as smooth as a new-born baby's. Nervously he felt his arms, his legs, his feet, his face—it was a miracle—the disease had gone. Jesus had touched him and Jesus had healed him. Jude fell on his knees in front of his Lord and praised God that he had at last been made clean. He was no longer an outcast.

THE VOYAGE OF THE GOOD SHIP CRISPIN

Introduction: This is a comic play in five episodes for performance to children. We used it as a daily serial during a Holiday Club, giving the final episode at a Family Service on the Sunday. It is a kind of allegory, based loosely on incidents in the life of the disciple Simon Peter. It deals with the recruitment of a crew by the Captain of the Good Ship Crispin, and their voyage to a treasure island. Clearly, the Captain is intended to represent Jesus, with the disciples Simon Peter, Philip, Andrew and Nathanael represented by Seaman Simon, Pip Squeak, Handy Andy and Fat Nat respectively. It will be enjoyed by children—especially if presented without inhibition, with over-the-top performances by the actors—but it will make little sense unless accompanied by some discussion and teaching. Although children will not necessarily follow every detail of the analogies implied in the story, the play nevertheless serves a useful purpose in exposing them to some of the concepts and emotions central to our understanding of the discipleship of Simon Peter and his companions.

EPISODE 1: Recruitment

Bible Base: John 1.35–49; John 6.60–69; Luke 9.57–62; Luke 14.18–20.

Explanation: This episode is based on the call of the disciples, and introduces the main characters, with their individual characteristics: the Captain, who should wear a distinctive naval cap of some sort (important for Episode 5); Seaman Simon, energetic and impatient; Pip Squeak, rather feeble and always threatening to be seasick; Fat Nat, overweight (plenty of cushions) and inclined to over-eating; and Handy Andy, reliable and practical. There is also reference to those who made excuses not to follow Jesus, and those who started but turned back because his teaching was too hard for them to accept.

Various props are needed to identify the times when the characters are on board ship; in particular, an anchor and a ship's wheel are required.

Cast: Announcer, The Captain, Seaman Simon, Handy Andy, Pip Squeak, Fat Nat, Jude, Levi, Cain.

(Seaman Simon, Handy Andy, Pip Squeak and Fat Nat sit round a table on one side of the stage, chatting. The Captain is over the other side, with Jude, Levi and Cain – they are stationary during opening scene.)

Announcer The Voyage of the Good Ship Crispin. Episode One. Four friends, Seaman Simon, Handy Andy, Fat Nat and Pip Squeak, are sitting in a cafe beside a harbour, talking.

Seaman Simon What we need round here is some action. We haven't been to sea for months.

Pip Squeak Been to see what? Been to see a film?

Seaman Simon Don't be such an idiot, Pip Squeak. Been to sea! You know, sea? Gurgle, gurgle, splash, splash, water, water everywhere, nor any drop to drink.

Fat Nat Did someone say drink? I don't mind if I do. A pint of rum will do nicely, thank you.

Handy Andy Seaman Simon's right, shipmates. What we need is a good ship to sail on, and a good captain we can rely on.

Fat Nat What I need, Handy Andy, is another one of those cream cakes. Can you pass me one?

Seaman Simon No wonder they call you Fat Nat! You'll make yourself sick!

Pip Squeak All this talk about going to sea makes me feel sick.

Fat Nat Well in that case, Pip Squeak, you won't be wanting that doughnut.

(He reaches out a hand, but gets it slapped by Seaman Simon. The Captain's group comes to life.)

Captain *(as though addressing a large crowd)* So, my friends, I set sail tomorrow. Volunteers are needed for the crew. Come along here at 7 am sharp, if you want to join me. *(Jude, Levi, Cain talk amongst themselves.)*

Seaman Simon I'm going out. Can't stand all this sitting around talking. See you later, shipmates.

(They bid him farewell. He wanders over to where the Captain is talking; Seaman Simon shows a lot of interest.)

Captain It'll be an exciting voyage, at times dangerous, and you'll have to trust me – but I'll be with you all the way. A voyage to a treasure island you could only have dreamed of. So, tomorrow, we sail. Will you join me on the Good Ship Crispin? You there, you want a good job on a good ship?

Levi I'd love to, but, er, I've got to go to a funeral tomorrow – my great aunt Agatha, so sudden . . . *(Exit.)*

Captain And what about you? You look like a strong young man . . .

Jude Why not. Seven o'clock tomorrow, right? I'll be there, Captain.

Captain And you, sir? Will you follow me?

Cain Well, I would, but, you see, I've just bought myself a cow, and at 7 o'clock tomorrow I shall have udder business to attend to. *(Exit.)*

Captain Well, men, spread the word—I need a crew. Tomorrow we sail—be here at seven!

Seaman Simon I'll be there, Captain—and I'll bring my brother, Handy Andy—and our friends, Pip Squeak and Fat Nat!

(Captain and Jude exit; Seaman Simon runs to tell others.)

Seaman Simon Great news, shipmates! I've found our ship—I've found our Captain! We sail tomorrow, 7 am. The Good Ship Crispin.

Handy Andy Well done, Simon! Where're we going?

(They begin to leave, talking, excitedly.)

Fat Nat What's the food like?

Pip Squeak Sailing? . . .Tomorrow? I think I'm going to be sick. *(They exit.)*

(The scene now changes to on board the Good Ship Crispin.)

Announcer The next morning. Just after seven.

(The Captain, Jude, Seaman Simon, Handy Andy, Pip Squeak, Fat Nat enter and set to work. Captain shouts orders, Crew respond energetically, running round doing imaginary tasks.)

Captain Splice the mainbrace!

Jude Mainbrace spliced, Cap'n.

Captain Tighten the sprongles!

Handy Andy Sprongles tightened, Cap'n.

Captain Loosen the springles!

Jude Springles loosened, Cap'n.

Captain Unshackle the rollocks!

Seaman Simon Rollocks unshackled, Cap'n.

Captain Wiggle the scroggles!

Handy Andy Scroggles wiggled, Cap'n.

Captain Agitate the oscillators!

Pip Squeak Oscillators agitated, Cap'n. Oh dear, I know I'm going to be seasick.

Captain Weigh the anchor!

Fat Nat *(lifting up an anchor)* Anchor weighed, Cap'n. Two hundred kilograms.

Jude *(looking exhausted)* Phew! I've had enough of this already. Too much like hard work with this Captain, if you ask me. I'm off *(begins to leave)*—have a good trip, folks. Think of me sitting at home with my feet up, and a pint of ale, in front of a nice warm log fire . . . *(Exit.)*

Captain And what about the rest of you? Will you leave also?

Seaman Simon Where could we go better than this? You're the Captain, you've got the ship. You know how to sail it. You know where you're going.

Pip Squeak, Handy Andy, Fat Nat We're with you, Captain!

Captain Right then, here we go, shipmates! The Good Ship Crispin is about to take you on a voyage you will never forget!

(Crew cheer: all exit.)

EPISODE 2: Forgiven

Bible Base: John 13.36–38, 18.15–18, 18.25–27, 21.15–19.

Explanation: This episode parallels Simon Peter's denial of the Lord and his subsequent reinstatement.

Cast: Announcer, The Captain, Seaman Simon, Handy Andy, Pip Squeak, Fat Nat, three people in cafe: A, B, C.

Announcer The Voyage of the Good Ship Crispin. Episode Two. The story so far. The Captain of the Good Ship Crispin has recruited Seaman Simon, Handy Andy, Fat Nat and Pip Squeak as crew on a voyage to a treasure island. They have set sail and are now on the high seas.

(Seaman Simon, Handy Andy, Pip Squeak, Fat Nat and the Captain are on board ship: the Captain is at the wheel; they improvise some comic business to do with the ship swaying from side to side, and Pip Squeak threatening to be sick; eventually the Captain calls out.)

Captain Attention, all members of the crew! *(Crew stand to attention, but have difficulty because of ship swaying.)* I don't mean stand to attention, I mean listen.

Pip Squeak Aye, aye, Cap'n.

Captain You, you, what?

Pip Squeak I, I . . . I am . . . feeling sick again, Captain.

Captain Now, listen all you men. We've been at sea for several days now, so we're going to put in to port tonight.

Fat Nat Did someone mention port? I don't mind if I do.

Captain *(ignoring this)* I shall want you to go ashore to get some supplies for the rest of the journey.

Seaman Simon Aye, aye, Cap'n.

Captain Now, you're doing it, Seaman Simon. Why has everyone started stuttering?

Fat Nat S..s..s..s..supplies, Cap'n? You mean things like fresh water, flour, fruit, vegetables, cheese *(getting more and more excited)*, biscuits, cream cakes, roly-poly puddings, jam tarts, ice cream sundaes, apple dumplings, black forest gateau, and loads and loads of lovely doughnuts!

Pip Squeak Stop it, Fat Nat. You're making me feel sick again.

Captain Thank you for your suggestions, Nat. But I think I'll put Seaman Simon in charge of the supplies. Right, every man to his station—we're approaching the harbour now. This is a very tricky approach, there are plenty of hazards just below the surface. Simon, you take the wheel. I'll guide you through. *(Simon takes the wheel downstage. Captain goes to the front of the ship, the others form a line from the Captain to Seaman Simon. The Captain calls out things like 'left hand down a bit'; these instructions are passed on up the line by the others, repeating the instructions word for word, until they reach Seaman Simon who also repeats them and acts accordingly. Eventually...)*

Captain Right, we're coming into the landing point now...drop anchor, Pip Squeak.

Pip Squeak Drop anchor, Pip Squeak!

Fat Nat Drop anchor, Pip Squeak!

Seaman Simon Drop anchor, Pip Squeak!

All except Pip Squeak Drop anchor, Pip Squeak!!! *(Pause)* Too late! *(They fall forward in a heap, acting as though the ship has come to a sudden halt. Eventually they sort themselves out...)*

Captain OK, men, you go ashore. Here's the list of supplies. Enjoy yourselves, but be back by midnight. Don't let me down.

Seaman Simon Let you down? After the way you steered us into this harbour—wow—that was really something! You're the sort of Captain we've always wanted—someone who knows what he's doing. Someone we can trust. So don't worry, we'll be back. You can be sure of that. You can rely on Seaman Simon.

(They begin to disembark.)

Handy Andy We're not going to leave you now, Captain.

Pip Squeak We're with you all the way, Captain.

Seaman Simon See you before the clock strikes twelve, Captain. We're your crew now. *(They exit.)*

Captain *(thoughtfully)* I hope so, Simon, I hope so. *(Exit.)*

Announcer Five minutes to midnight. With all the supplies safely purchased, Seaman Simon has wandered into a cafe for a drink. *(Seaman Simon is now sitting in a cafe, aside from three others, A, B and C; Seaman Simon gets increasingly embarrassed at the overheard conversation.)*

A Have you seen that clapped-out old junk that's pulled into the harbour? *(Much hilarity.)*

B The Good Ship Crispin they call it! Crisp-in! What's it carrying? Ten thousand packets of salt and vinegar flavour?

C The fellow in charge, what do you know about him?

A Calls himself . . . the Captain.

B Clapped-out would be a better name!

C Has he got a crew?

B Why, you thinking of joining him?

C Not likely! No, I just wondered who would ever join up with an outfit like that.

A Oh yes, he's got a crew. I saw them coming ashore this afternoon. In fact . . . I say, see that fellow over there . . . *(calling to Seaman Simon)*. Excuse me, shipmate . . . *(Seaman Simon turns away, ignoring A)* . . . excuse me, I'm talking to you. Aren't you one of the crew of that wreck, the Crispin?

Seaman Simon No, I'm not. Now just clear off and let me finish my drink in peace.

B I bet he is one of them. Look at him, he's not from around these parts. *(With heavy sarcasm)* What's it like, shipmate, working for 'the Captain'?

Seaman Simon I don't know who you're talking about. Just leave me in peace, will you!

(The Captain enters, unnoticed.)

C *(teasing Seaman Simon, singing)* 'On the good ship Lollipop, on the good ship Lollipop . . .'

A Come on, mate, you can tell us all about it, we won't laugh . . . much!

Seaman Simon *(really angry now)* For the last time, I have never been on this ship you call the Crispin, I never want to go on it, I've never heard of the Captain, whoever he might be, and as far as I'm concerned, the three of you, the Good Ship Crispin, and the Captain, can all get lost! *(A clock begins to strike twelve. He stands up, in a fury, starts to storm out and comes face to face with the Captain.)*

Seaman Simon Captain!

Captain Simon.

Seaman Simon Oh, Captain, I'm sorry. Forgive me. I didn't... *(He falls to the ground, breaks down, and stays there while the clock finishes striking twelve.)*

Captain Come this way, Seaman Simon.

(He takes Seaman Simon by the hand, leads him back towards the ship. A, B, C exit.)

Captain I have a new job for you, Simon.

Seaman Simon What, a new job? After the way I let you down... you're still prepared to have me in the crew? I'll do anything, Captain–scrub the decks, washing up, make cream cakes for Fat Nat, clear up after Pip Squeak's been sick–anything... if you will really let me stay!

Captain I was impressed by the way you handled the wheel as we came into harbour this afternoon. I'm going to make you my number two, Simon.

Seaman Simon But... back there, in the cafe... I said...

Captain Simon, when we get back on board I want you to take the wheel.

Seaman Simon Aye, aye, Cap'n.

Captain You're stuttering again, Simon!

Seaman Simon *(laughing)* Shall we set sail... Captain?

Captain Aye, aye... Lieutenant.

Captain and Seaman Simon All aboard! *(Exit.)*

EPISODE 3: Progress

Bible Base: Acts 1–4; 1 Peter 2.2, 5.10.

Explanation: Simon Peter, who let the Lord down so dreadfully, was later transformed by the power of his Spirit, along with the other disciples, as described so vividly in the opening chapters of Acts. Christ's own words to them were fulfilled: 'You will receive power when the Holy Spirit comes upon you.' Later, Peter would write his first letter, and, from his own experience, could encourage young Christians to 'grow up in your salvation,' and reassure them that 'God himself will restore you and make you strong, firm and steadfast.' This episode of the serial play focuses on the way in which Jesus can transform and empower his followers for the work he has given them to do.

Cast: Announcer, The Captain, Seaman Simon, Handy Andy, Pip Squeak, Fat Nat.

Announcer The Voyage of the Good Ship Crispin. Episode Three. The story so far. The Captain of the Good Ship Crispin has recruited Seaman Simon, Handy Andy, Fat Nat and Pip Squeak as crew on a voyage to a treasure island. After letting the Captain down, Seaman Simon has been forgiven, reinstated as a member of the crew, and promoted to lieutenant.
(Seaman Simon, Handy Andy and the Captain are on board ship: Seaman Simon is at the wheel; Pip Squeak and Fat Nat are below deck, i.e. out of sight.)

Seaman Simon *(steering the ship, singing)* 'Hey, ho and up she rises, hey, ho and up she rises, hey, ho and up she rises, ear-ly in the morning . . .'

Handy Andy You feeling all right, Simon?

Seaman Simon Sure am, shipmate. Ah, yes, this is the life for me. A sunny day on board ship, the wind on your back, sea air in your lungs, the smell of salt water all round you. Life is good here on the Good Ship Crispin.

Captain It's good to see you doing your job so well now, Lieutenant.

Seaman Simon Aye, aye, Cap'n. *(Sings)* 'A life on the ocean wave, a life on the ocean wave . . .'

Captain Sorry to interrupt your wonderful recital, Simon, but I fear we have some nasty weather coming up. Look over there *(They look into the distance)*. We'd better get the rest of the crew to their stations. Where are they, by the way? Shouldn't they be here on deck?

Seaman Simon Pip Squeak is down below lying on his bunk, being seasick again. He's useless even in this good weather–how he'll cope in a storm, I can't imagine.

Handy Andy And Fat Nat is in the galley . . .

All three together . . . eating doughnuts!

Seaman Simon He's getting so fat, he can hardly get around the deck these days.

Captain Well, call them on deck, Andy. They are going to have to do something if we're going to ride out that storm. It looks really bad to me.

Handy Andy Aye, aye, Cap'n. *(Shouts)* All hands on deck. *(Goes to door and shouts even louder)* All hands on deck. *(Pip Squeak and Fat Nat enter, crawling. Fat Nat is even fatter– more cushions! Pip Squeak is looking decidedly sick.)*

Seaman Simon What are you doing down there? Stand up when the Captain wants to speak to you. *(They stand.)*

Pip Squeak But he said all hands on deck. *(Gestures with his hands.)* Oh dear, I do feel sick.

Fat Nat And I feel hungry. I was halfway through my mid-morning coffee and doughnut break when you called.

Handy Andy So presumably you still had another twenty-five dough-nuts to go.

Captain OK, men, enough of this bickering. We've got serious work to do. There's a storm brewing up ahead of us. We're all going to have to pull our weight . . . *(looks at Fat Nat)* . . . perhaps I'll rephrase that . . . we're all going to have to play our part to get through it safely. If anyone fails us, we could lose the ship. We could lose our lives. I'm depending on each one of you.

Pip Squeak A storm? Oh, no. That means that the boat will go up and down, and side to side, rocking and tilting and swaying and . . . oh dear, I'm bound to be seasick. I'll be no use to you at all, Captain. Sorry. You'll have to manage without me.

Captain *(looking straight at Pip Squeak)* Now, listen, Pip Squeak. You don't have to be seasick all the time. I shall be giving you a job to do, and I shall see that you do it. Do you understand?

Pip Squeak But, I . . . I . . . aye, aye, Cap'n.

Captain And you, Nat. You're too fat. I am putting you on a strict diet. No more doughnuts. No more cream cakes. No more jam tarts or roly-poly puddings.

Fat Nat But I'll never be able to manage, Captain. I know I'm a useless seaman like this, but, if I don't get my daily dose of doughnuts . . . Please, Captain. When the storm comes, I'll just crawl into the galley . . .

Captain Nat, you have your job to do. Forget about your doughnuts. If you're going to follow me, then my word must be more important to you than anything else. You can manage. Look at me when I'm talking to you! Listen to what I am saying. You will be an able-bodied seaman. Trust me. You can do it.

Seaman Simon Storm's starting, Captain! All men to their stations. Fasten down the hatches! Here we go. *(Lots of action and sound effects; improvise the effects of a storm. Fat Nat gradually gets moving, but with difficulty. All the following conversation is shouted over the noise of the storm. Eventually . . .)*

Captain It's no good, we'll have to lose some cargo. We're too heavy. Nat, go below and see what we can dispose of . . . hurry . . . we're taking too much water on board!

Fat Nat Aye, aye, Cap'n. *(Goes below.)*

Seaman Simon Captain, I've had it! Someone else'll have to take over the wheel. Hurry! I can't hold it much longer!

Captain Pip, take over from Simon at the wheel.

Pip Squeak What me, Captain? But if I go up there on the bridge, with all that swaying, I'll just be . . . *(holds his tummy, puts hand over his mouth)*.

Captain Pip, you can do it. Go on. We're depending on you. Trust me!

Pip Squeak Oh dear . . .

Seaman Simon *(sounding desperate)* I've had it, Captain, sorry! *(He collapses: the Captain goes across and attends to him.)*

Pip Squeak *(talking to himself)* Take the wheel, eh. Go up there . . . on the bridge. Right. The Captain said I can do it, so . . . I can do it . . . Aye, aye, Cap'n!

(Pip Squeak takes over the wheel. Fat Nat returns with huge sacks which he starts ditching overboard.)

Handy Andy Good work, Nat! That should cut down our cargo weight. Those sacks look as though they weigh a ton!

Fat Nat They do–but I won't!

Handy Andy What d'you mean?

Fat Nat Can't you see what's in them?

Handy Andy Well, I'll be . . . doughnuts!

Captain Well done, Nat! Well done, everyone. Now hold on, men, we're nearly through the worst of it. The storm's subsiding. *(Sounds of storm and swaying actions gradually lessen, then silence.)*

Pip Squeak We made it!

Handy Andy Three cheers for the Captain! Hip, hip . . . *(etc.)*.

Captain Three cheers for you as well, men. You all turned up trumps. Well, Pip, how're you feeling?

Pip Squeak Fine, Cap'n. Just fine. You take a rest, I'll look after the ship.

Captain And you, Nat? It's gone four o'clock–isn't it time you were sneaking off to the galley for a little something?

Fat Nat No thanks, Captain. I've got work to do on deck, clearing up after the storm.

Captain Righto, men. I'm handing over to you, then. I'll be going below for a rest. OK? *(Exit.)*

Pip Squeak, Fat Nat, Handy Andy, Seaman Simon Aye, aye, Cap'n! *(Sing, dance, with actions.)* 'We're riding along on the crest of a wave, and the sun is in the sky, two, three, four! All our eyes on the distant horizon, look out for passers-by! We'll do the hailing, while other ships are out a-sailing. We're riding along on the crest of the wave, and the world is ours! *(Exit, waving to audience.)*

EPISODE 4: Pirates!

Bible Base: Acts 12.1–17; John 16.33; 1 Peter 1.3–9; Romans 7.14–25.

Explanation: In this episode the crew are taken prisoner by pirates, led by the evil Black Patch, but are then saved by the intervention of the Captain. There is a parallel in the miraculous escape of Peter from prison in Acts 12. The focus for discussion of the episode should be the ongoing battle between good and evil in the life of the Christian. When the Christian cries: 'Who will rescue me?' the answer is emphatic: 'Jesus Christ our Lord!' (Romans 7.25). We have Christ's own words in John 16: 'In the world you will have trouble, but take heart. I have overcome the world.' Peter, in his first letter, would later write of salvation as both a present experience: '. . .you are receiving the goal of your faith, the salvation of your souls;' and a future hope: '. . .you, who through faith are shielded by God's power until the coming of the salvation that is ready to be revealed.'

Cast: Announcer, The Captain, Seaman Simon, Handy Andy, Pip Squeak, Fat Nat, Black Patch and assorted pirates.

Announcer The Voyage of the Good Ship Crispin. Episode Four. The story so far. The Captain of the Good Ship Crispin has recruited Seaman Simon, Handy Andy, Fat Nat and Pip Squeak as crew on a voyage to a treasure island. After letting the Captain down, Seaman Simon has been forgiven, reinstated as a member of the crew, and promoted to lieutenant. After the storm, Pip Squeak has overcome his fear of seasickness, and Fat Nat has given up doughnuts. All are now useful members of the crew and the Captain is able to hand over to them the ruining of the ship.

Handy Andy *(enters and checks Announcer's script)* Running, not ruining!

Announcer Sorry, sorry. The Captain is able to hand over to them the running of the ship.

(The Captain is at the wheel of the Crispin.)

Captain Rise and shine, shipmates. All hands on deck. Lieutenant Simon, Pip Squeak, Handy Andy . . .Flat Nat!

(Seaman Simon, Pip Squeak, Handy Andy, Fat Nat enter one at a time, responding 'Aye, aye, Cap'n', and stand in a line, swaying

gently from side to side. Fat Nat has lost a lot of weight and is now known as Flat Nat!)

Captain Take over, Lieutenant. I'm going below for the next shift. The ship is in your hands, men. *(Exit.)*

Seaman Simon Aye, aye, Captain. *(Takes the wheel; they sail blissfully for a while, whistling, busy about the ship. Then . . .)*

Handy Andy *(looking through telescope, and calling in a monotone announcer's voice, cupping hands over mouth)* Ship ahoy! Vessel approaching fast three to four nautical miles to starboard, bearing approximately north fifty degrees east, speed twenty-five knots.

Pip Squeak I beg your pardon?

Handy Andy There's a ship coming, fast, over there!

Pip Squeak *(imitating Handy Andy's announcer's voice)* There's a coming ship, fast, over there. There's a ship coming, fast, over there. There's a ship coming, fast, over there. Don't panic.

Handy Andy *(looking through telescope)* Shiver my timbers, the skull and crossbones!

Pip Squeak *(announcer's voice)* Shiver his timbers. The skull and crossbones. Skull and crossbones! Don't panic. Don't panic! Skull and crossbones.

Seaman Simon Looks like trouble, men. This could mean . . . pirates!

Pip Squeak Pirates! Panic! Panic!

Seaman Simon OK, men, action stations! Take your weapons. They're coming alongside! *(Action.)*

Fat Nat Here they come! Defend the Crispin!

All Defend the Crispin!

(Enter Black Patch and pirates – improvise a battle – much gnashing of teeth, clashing of swords, etc; eventually all four members of the crew are taken prisoner and tied up. Black Patch takes the wheel!)

Black Patch *(sounding very evil)* Ha, ha, ha! Ho, ho, ho! Now this ship is mine! You are my prisoners. And at day break I shall take great delight in chopping off your ears to feed my parrot, chopping off your fingers to feed my men, and then throwing the rest of you overboard to feed the sharks! Ha, ha, ha! Now where do you keep all your supplies? Come on, speak up! Who is your captain?

(The Captain enters behind Black Patch.)

Captain I am the Captain, Black Patch.

Black Patch *(turns)* What! You? The Captain!

Captain Yes, it is I, the Captain. *(Advances confidently, pointing.)* And you, Black Patch, will put down your sword, order your men to put down their weapons, you will untie my crew, and you will take your motley crowd of pirates off my ship, and you will do it now!

(Black Patch and pirates respond accordingly: they exit, defeated.)

Crew We're free!

Pip Squeak How did you do that, Captain?

Handy Andy They just gave up and went!

Fat Nat And you only spoke to them—you didn't even have a weapon!

Captain One day, men, you will understand. There is a power which does not depend upon a sword, there is an authority which does not derive from weapons, there is a force for good which evil cannot resist. And that power can be yours, if you follow me and trust me.

Seaman Simon We will follow you and trust you, Captain. Right to the end.

Handy Andy What now, Captain?

Captain Well, men, I have news for you. We are nearing the end of our voyage. Tomorrow we shall be arriving . . . at our destination! *(All cheer and then exit.)*

EPISODE 5: Saved!

Bible Base: 1 Peter 2.24, 3.18.

Explanation: In the final episode of the play the crew are safe on the treasure island, after a violent storm and a shipwreck, in which the Captain laid down his life in order that they might be saved. This is obviously designed to introduce the idea of Christ laying down his life on the cross for our eternal salvation. As Peter himself wrote, 'For Christ died for our sins once for all, the righteous for the unrighteous, to bring you to God.' The crew review the story in the previous episodes in short flashbacks, which are pre-recorded. Clearly it would not be appropriate to introduce anything comparable to the resurrection into this play, but there is just a hint of this idea in the final line.

Cast: Announcer, Seaman Simon, Handy Andy, Pip Squeak, Fat Nat. Various voices pre-recorded.

Announcer The Voyage of the Good Ship Crispin. Episode Five. The story so far. The Captain of the Good Ship Crispin recruited

Seaman Simon, Handy Andy, Fat Nat and Pip Squeak as crew on a voyage to a treasure island. After many adventures on the high seas, they have finally arrived at a wonderful island. The four crew members are relaxing in the sunshine on the beach, recalling their adventures.

(The four crew members are on the beach of the island. Seaman Simon has the ship's log. Various props litter the beach, including the anchor, the ship's wheel and the Captain's cap.)

Seaman Simon Well, shipmates, what do you think of this place? Pretty neat, eh?

Handy Andy Wonderful! This morning I discovered how to get waves in your hair.

Seaman Simon How's that?

Handy Andy Lie on the beach when the tide's coming in. Pass me another glass of coconut milk, Pip Squeak.

Fat Nat We'll never go hungry on this island, will we?

Pip Squeak You mean, because of all the sand-which-is here?

Seaman Simon You're not missing your doughnuts too much then, Nat?

Fat Nat Oh no—the Captain said he would turn me into an able-bodied seaman, and he did. I'm not Fat Nat any more! *(The others look very sad at the mention of the Captain.)* What's the matter? Oh, yes, of course. I'm sorry to mention the Captain.

Seaman Simon That's all right, Nat. If we tell the truth, we're all thinking about him, all the time. *(Picks up the Captain's cap.)* Remembering what it was like, when he was with us. *(Puts down the cap. Starts to browse through ship's log.)*

Fat Nat Anyone want to listen to one of my eight favourite gramophone records? I just happen to have them with me . . .

Handy Andy Not just now, thanks, Nat. What's that book you've got there, Simon?

Seaman Simon It's the ship's log. I managed to rescue it . . .

Pip Squeak That's good. We need a few logs for the fire tonight.

Seaman Simon Not that sort of log, Pip Squeak. It's the ship's diary. This is a record of everything that happened on the voyage of the Good Ship Crispin. I was thinking of making just one final entry . . .

Handy Andy Let's have a look. *(Takes the log and reads.)* Listen to this . . . '22nd August: a crew of strong but rather foolish men were recruited for the Good Ship Crispin—Seaman Simon,

Handy Andy, Pip Squeak and Fat Nat...' It's all here—the whole story, everything that happened.

Seaman Simon I'll always remember that day when I heard the Captain for the first time . . .

RECORDING 1

Captain So, my friends, I set sail tomorrow. Volunteers are needed for the crew. Come along here at 7 am sharp, if you want to join me. It'll be an exciting voyage, at times dangerous, and you'll have to trust me—I'll be with you all the way. A voyage to a treasure island you could only have dreamed of. So, tomorrow we sail. Will you join me on the Good Ship Crispin?

Fat Nat We went along with you when you told us about the Captain— but once we met him for ourselves, we knew we had to be in his crew. But do you remember that guy who started out with us. He didn't last long, did he . . .

RECORDING 2

Jude Phew. I've had enough of this already. Too much like hard work with this Captain, if you ask me. I'm off . . .

Captain And what about the rest of you? Will you leave also?

Seaman Simon Where could we go better than this? You're the Captain, you've got the ship. You know how to sail it. You know where you're going.

Pip Squeak, Handy Andy, Fat Nat We're with you, Captain!

Seaman Simon Full of fine words, wasn't I? *(Takes log, looks through it.)* Do you remember when we landed for supplies?—'I'll be back before midnight, Captain,' I said. 'You can rely on me. I'll stick with you for ever.' Huh! Typical!

Fat Nat Don't torment yourself, Simon.

Seaman Simon But I let him down, didn't I? When those guys in the cafe started teasing me about being one of his crew members, I just snapped.

RECORDING 3

Seaman Simon For the last time, I have never been on this ship you call the Crispin, I never want to go on it, I've never heard of the Captain, whoever he might be, and as far as I'm concerned, the three of you, the Good Ship Crispin, and the Captain, can all get lost! *(A clock begins to strike twelve.)*

Seaman Simon Captain!

Captain Simon.

Seaman Simon Oh, Captain, I'm sorry. Forgive me. I didn't ...
> *(He breaks down, while the clock finishes striking twelve.)*

Captain Come this way, Seaman Simon. I have a new job for you.

Seaman Simon The way he was willing to forgive me—I couldn't believe it—and yet he really did forgive me! I was never the same after that!

Pip Squeak He changed me, as well. Do you remember what I used to be like?

All together *(mocking Pip Squeak)* 'I think I'm going to be seasick!'

Pip Squeak But when that first storm came, suddenly I found a new strength. Do you remember that terrible storm ...

Seaman Simon *(looks in log)* Will we ever forget it? It's all here in the log.

RECORDING 4

> *(Storm noises.)*

Seaman Simon Captain, I've had it! Someone else'll have to take over the wheel. Hurry! I can't hold it much longer!

Captain Pip, take over from Simon at the wheel.

Pip Squeak What, me, Captain? But if I go up there on the bridge, with all that swaying, I'll just be seasick.

Captain Pip, you can do it. Go on. We're depending on you. Trust me!

Pip Squeak Oh dear ...

Seaman Simon *(sounding desperate)* I've had it, Captain, sorry!

Pip Squeak Take the wheel, eh. Go up there ... on the bridge. Right. The Captain said I can do it, so I can do it ... Aye, aye, Cap'n!

Handy Andy And I don't think you were ever seasick again after that.

Pip Squeak I didn't have time to be seasick. Too much to do around the ship! The Captain always seemed to have another useful job for me to be getting on with.

Handy Andy You know the thing that surprised me was that in the end he was even able to hand over the running of the ship to us.

Seaman Simon But we were pretty hopeless when those pirates attacked us, weren't we?

Pip Squeak Black Patch and his evil gang! I thought we'd had it. But do you remember what happened after we were all taken prisoner and tied up? ...

RECORDING 5

Black Patch Ha, ha, ha! Now you are my prisoners. Now, come on, speak up! Who is your captain?

Captain I am the Captain, Black Patch.

Black Patch What! You? The Captain!

Captain Yes, it is I, the Captain. And you, Black Patch, will put down your sword, order your men to put down their weapons, you will untie my crew, and you will take your motley crowd of pirates off my ship, and you will do it now!

Fat Nat And they just went! It was amazing. One word from the Captain and they turned and ran!

Seaman Simon Then the next morning we sighted the island. But before we could land we ran into that second terrifying storm.

Fat Nat It was as though all the forces of evil, all the powers of darkness, were trying to stop us getting here. I've never known a storm like it. The ship didn't stand a chance.

RECORDING 6

Captain *(shouting over storm noises)* Simon, I will take the wheel. The ship's struck a rock! She's going down. Andy, Nat, get the lifeboat ready. You men take the lifeboat. Go on, Pip. Do as I say! Take the lifeboat. Now. She's going down! I'll hold the ship steady while you men get to safety. Go on! You must get to the island. Quick, men – you can make it. You will be saved, if you go . . . if you go now . . .

Fat Nat *(takes log book and reads)* 'As we approached the island, a wild and evil storm came upon us. The ship struck a huge rock. The Captain kept her steady while we took the lifeboat to safety. Those were his orders. We obeyed. The ship and the Captain went down.' *(Pause)* What else is there to say, Simon?

Seaman Simon *(takes the log and writes)* 'I, Seaman Simon, am writing this the final entry in the log of the Good Ship Crispin. We know this to be the truth. The Captain laid down his life for the sake of the crew; he died so that we could be brought to safety.' *(He closes the log. They are silent for a while.)* Come on, men. Let's go for a walk along this beautiful beach. *(They start to leave. Seaman Simon is the last to go – he picks up the Captain's cap and looks at it thoughtfully.)* And keep your eyes open. You never know . . . maybe . . . *(Exit.)*

Other titles by Derek Haylock published by National Society/Church House Publishing:

Acts for Apostles

Drama for Disciples

The National Society

The National Society (Church of England) for Promoting Religious Education is the voluntary body, founded in 1811, which established the first network of schools in England and Wales based on the national Church. It now supports all those involved in Christian education—diocesan education teams, teachers, governors, clergy, students and parents—with the resources of its RE Centres, archives, courses and conferences. The Society publishes a wide range of books, pamphlets and audio-visual items, and two magazines, *Crosscurrent* and *Together*. It can give legal and administrative advice for schools and colleges and award grants for Church school building projects.

The Society works in close association with the General Synod Board of Education, and with the Division for Education of the Church in Wales, but greatly values the independent status which enables it to take initiatives in developing new work. The Society has a particular concern for Christian goals and values in education as a whole.

For details of corporate, associate and individual membership of the Society contact: The Promotions Secretary, The National Society, Church House, Great Smith Street, London SW1P 3NZ. Telephone 071-222 1672.